Research Reports ESPRIT

Project 2463 · ARGOSI · Volume 1

Edited in cooperation with
the Commission of the European Communities

R.A. Day D.A. Duce
J.R. Gallop D.C. Sutcliffe (Eds.)

Integration of Graphics and OSI Standards

Springer-Verlag

Berlin Heidelberg New York
London Paris Tokyo
Hong Kong Barcelona
Budapest

Editors

Robert A. Day, David A. Duce, Julian R. Gallop, Dale C. Sutcliffe
Rutherford Appleton Laboratory
Chilton, Didcot, Oxon OX11 0QX, UK

ESPRIT Project 2463 "Applications-Related Graphics and OSI Standards Integration (ARGOSI)" belongs to the Subprogramme "Advanced Business and Home Systems – Peripherals" of ESPRIT, the European Specific Programme for Research and Development in Information Technology supported by the Commission of the European Communities.

The project arose from the recognition that within ISO/IEC, as elsewhere, standards for computer graphics and standards for Open Systems Interconnection have been largely developed in isolation and little serious attention has been paid to issues of integration. The overall aims of the project were twofold: firstly to advance the state of the art in the transfer of graphical information across international networks and secondly to improve the quality and applicability of standards in this area.

Partners in the project were:

COSI (Italy), FhG-IGD (Germany), GESI (Italy), GMD-FOKUS (Germany), Hitec (Greece), INRIA (France), Laser-Scan (UK), Rutherford Appleton Laboratory (UK), Tecsiel (Italy), Thomson-CSF (France), University of East Anglia (UK)

UNIX is a registered Trademark of AT&T.

CR Subject Classification (1991): I.3.2, C.2.0–2

ISBN 3-540-57015-2 Springer-Verlag Berlin Heidelberg New York
ISBN 0-387-57015-2 Springer-Verlag New York Berlin Heidelberg

Publication No. EUR 15112 EN of the
Commission of the European Communities, Dissemination of Scientific and
Technical Knowledge Unit, Directorate-General Information Technologies
and Industries, and Telecommunications, Luxembourg

LEGAL NOTICE
Neither the Commission of the European Communities nor any person acting on behalf of the Commission is responsible for the use which might be made of the following information.

© ECSC-EEC-EAEC, Brussels-Luxembourg, 1993
Printed in Germany

Typesetting: Camera-ready by authors
45/3140 – 543210 – Printed on acid-free paper

Preface

The offices of GMD-FOKUS in Berlin provided the venue for a meeting in December 1987 which signalled the birth of the ARGOSI project. The proposal gradually took shape over the following months, and after merging with another project proposal in the field of standardization of computer graphics, finally received funding from the Esprit programme in March 1989. The project stemmed from a recognition of the importance of computer graphics as an enabling technology in many application areas, and of the need to build bridges between computer graphics and telecommunications. The overall aims of the project were twofold:

- Advance the state of the art in the transfer of graphical information across international networks.
- Improve quality and applicability of standards in this area.

This book records the key results of the project and the contributions the project has made to standardization related to the transfer of graphical information across open networks. Contributions have included a demonstration of a prototype application – a road transport information system running over public international data networks – shown at the Esprit '91 exhibition, the standardization of a new FTAM document type allowing structured access to graphical information (represented according to the Computer Graphics Metafile (CGM) standard) and major contributions to a mapping of the X-Windows protocol onto an OSI stack. The project also organized two international workshops, the first on Graphics and Communications, and the second on Distributed Window Systems.

The editors of this volume wish to place on record, on behalf of the whole project team, their thanks to all the project members who have contributed to this work, in particular to the managers of the project, Laurent Mistral and Michel Vernay, and also to Jochem Bisser, who did so much to create the ambience of the project and to engender a team spirit amongst the researchers.

R.A. Day D.A. Duce
J.R. Gallop D.C. Sutcliffe

August 1993

Table of Contents

1 Overview of Project

1.1 Introduction

Esprit (European Strategic Programme for Research into Information Technology) Project 2463, ARGOSI – Applications Related Graphics and OSI Standards Integration, started on 1 March 1989 and was of 3 years duration. Eleven organizations were involved throughout the project:

Prime Contractor	Thomson-CSF	France
Partners	INRIA	France
	RAL	UK
	Hitec	Greece
	Tecsiel	Italy
	COSI	Italy
	GMD-FOKUS	Germany
Associated Partners	Laser-Scan	UK
	FhG-IGD	Germany
	GESI	Italy
	University of East Anglia	UK

1.2 Initial Objectives

The project arose from the recognition that within ISO/IEC, as elsewhere, standards for computer graphics and standards for Open Systems Interconnection have been largely developed in isolation and little serious attention has been paid to issues of integration. The overall aims of the project were twofold:

- Advance the state of the art in the transfer of graphical information across international networks.

- Improve quality and applicability of standards in this area.

These aims were to be achieved through fulfillment of four specific objectives:

(1) The development of software tools and packages to assist in the construction of applications which use graphical transfer over wide-area networks. This will be the basis for the development of marketable products in this area.
(2) An improvement of both the quality and applicability of Standards in the area of graphics and of the application of OSI standards to the transfer of graphical objects.
(3) The development of a detailed understanding of how to construct systems which use Graphics and OSI networking. This understanding will be applicable across a wide range of applications domains.
(4) An investigation into the validity of currently available wide-area networking facilities via a practical demonstration involving a prototype within a suitable application domain.

The project plan explained the basic methodology for the project in the following way.

- *Identification and classification of application areas*. The initial objective will be to identify the range of applications to be considered within the project. The range will be selected from application areas of current commercial and scientific importance and also areas expected to become important within the duration of the project and beyond. Once identified, these applications will be classified according to their graphics requirements and the networking services needed for those graphics. These requirements and services will be matched to the emerging family of graphics and OSI standards.
- *Choice for a prototype application demonstration*. Classes of applications will be selected for prototyping and demonstration over wide-area OSI networks. Where implementations of the required graphics standards and networking services are not available, these will be produced by the project. Further classes of application will be studied in detail to see how their graphics and networking services could be provided and whether they could be met by existing standards.
- *Experimentation*. While the initial studies and classifications are taking place, OSI connectivity will be established between partners in the respective partners' country through national networks. The consortium will then implement a prototype application on these links. The prototype application will enable the evaluation of the integration of existing and forthcoming graphics (e.g. CGM, CGI) and OSI (e.g. X400, FTAM) standards.
- *Services Identification*. The studies are expected to identify graphics requirements and network services that cannot be achieved by the existing standards in the fields working in unison or that cannot be satisfied by the present generation of standards at all.

- *Standardization Proposals and Recommendations*. These observations will be reported to the ISO/IEC and Application Profile Committees and recommendations made on the harmonization of existing standards and requirements that need to be met by the next generation of standards.

The workplan of the project was structured as shown in Table 1.1.

Table 1.1. Project Workplan

	Workpackage		Tasks
1	Classification	1.1	Classification of applications
2	Connectivity	2.1	X25 Connectivity and evaluation
3	Standards Activities	3.1 3.2	Participation in standards activities Study of services needed
4	Prototype Application	4.1 4.2 4.3 4.4 4.5 4.6	Specification Generate application OSI Service implementation Graphics implementation Integration and demonstration Evaluation
5	Final Report	5.1	Final report
6	Management	6.1	Management

An outline bar chart showing the timings of these activities appears in Fig. 1.1. The project was expected to make an impact in a number of ways:

(1) *Knowledge*: when the project started, there was little understanding of the requirements which graphics place on networking in terms of the particular networking services required to transfer graphical information across networks. Such requirements arise, for example, because of the structure inherent in graphical information and the need to access subunits within an overall structure.

(2) *Standardization*: international standardization activities are seen as a key mechanism for achieving coherence and interoperability in an otherwise fragmented area. The contribution of the ARGOSI project to standardization activities was to be to identify requirements for future graphics and networking standards and make appropriate inputs to the standardization committees concerned. The organizations involved in the project had a long tradition of contributing independently to graphics and networking standardization. ARGOSI provided the opportunity for these organizations to work together in the standards-making process and so to form the nucleus around which a more coordinated and coherent European input could be made to the international process.

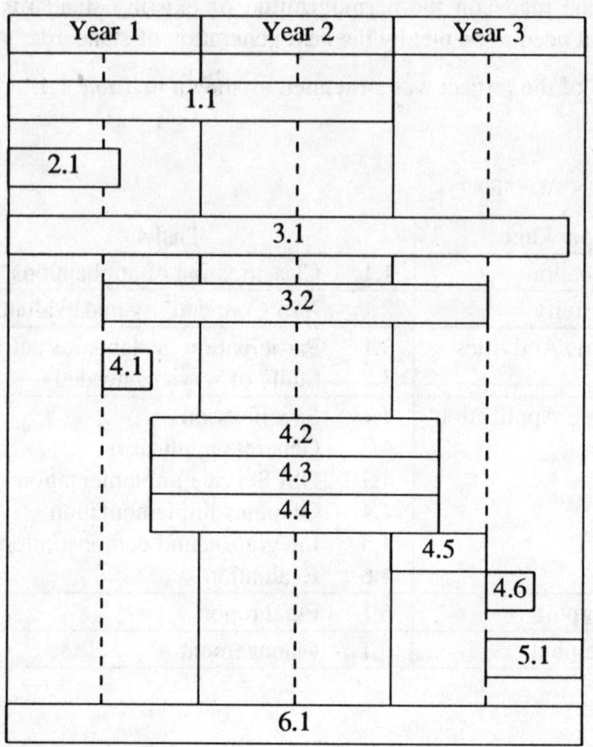

Fig. 1.1. Project Bar Chart

(3) *Industry*: From an industry standpoint the project set out to demonstrate what could be achieved in distributed graphics using existing international public data networks (PSPDNs). This would point the way to what could be expected as better international PSPDNs became available in the future and to the requirements for such facilities from applications. To demonstrate the state of the art, a prototype application was to be constructed.

(4) *Commercial*: the project was to develop software tools for graphics and networking services which would form the basis directly, or indirectly, of commercial products. The prototype application demonstrator would also generate knowledge and experience of how to (and equally importantly, how not to) build distributed graphics applications using ISO/IEC standards.

1.3 Related Work

1.3.1 Graphics Standards

Standardization activities have existed in computer graphics since the early 1970's in the International Organization for Standardization (ISO) and subsequently in ISO/IEC (International Electrotechnical Commission). The ISO/IEC family of standards covers a broad range of graphics requirements from application program interfaces for the generation and manipulation of 3D graphics to device level interfaces for the transfer of graphical information:

(1) *Application Program Interface (API) Standards*: these define a programming interface for applications. The first of these was the Graphical Kernel System (GKS – ISO 7942), followed by GKS-3D (ISO/IEC 8805), PHIGS and PHIGS PLUS (ISO/IEC 9592).
(2) *Metafile and Archive Standards*: these define representations of graphics for storage and transfer. The Computer Graphics Metafile for the storage and transfer of picture description information (CGM – ISO 8632) and Parts 2 and 3 of PHIGS (which specify the PHIGS Archive File) are of this type.
(3) *Device Interface Standards*: these cover the requirements for interfaces between device drivers and graphics devices. Interface techniques for dialogues with graphical devices (commonly known as CGI – ISO/IEC 9636) addresses these requirements.
(4) *Language Binding Standards*: API and device interface standards are defined independently of particular programming languages. Interfaces to programming languages are defined in separate standards.
(5) *Framework Standards*: included in this category are projects to develop a standard for a reference model for computer graphics and a standard for conformance and testing of graphics standards.

The current standards are described in Arnold and Duce.[1]

The next section describes some attempts at distributed implementations of the first application program interface standard, GKS, which have appeared in the literature, the use of networks for the transfer of static picture description information, along with more recent experience of distributed window systems.

1.3.2 Examples of Distributed Graphics Systems

GKS Implementations. GKS is an ISO standard for a 2D graphics system providing both graphical output and input. It is defined independently of programming languages, as a set of abstract functions and data types. Language bindings have been standardized for Fortran, Pascal and Ada (ISO 8651).

Full descriptions of GKS appear in books by Hopgood et al.[9] and Enderle et al.[6] The key concept to device independence in GKS is the *workstation* concept. A workstation in GKS consists of zero or one display surface and zero or more input devices plus associated software. The GKS idea of a workstation is an abstraction from physical hardware, which allows different graphics devices to be treated within GKS in a consistent way. A major difference from many earlier graphics systems is that GKS allows more than one workstation to be in use simultaneously. For example, an operator may be interacting with different parts of a design through different interactive displays.

The paper by Duce and Hopgood[4] includes a survey of implementation philosophies for GKS. Although this survey is rather dated, little has appeared in the literature since then. GKS was not designed with distributed implementation specifically in mind, but some distributed implementations have emerged. GKS does not have a well-defined internal interface between the device independent (DI) front-end part of GKS which the application program calls and that part of GKS, the device dependent (DD) part, which is responsible for the interface to devices. Devices vary widely in their capabilities and the implementation philosophy has to accommodate this.

Distributed GKS implementations typically insert a network connection between the device independent front-end part and the device dependent parts, in other words, the front-end runs on a separate host to the host(s) to which the output and input device(s) are attached. This raises two problems:

(1) Some of the GKS data structures held in the front-end need to be accessed by workstations.

(2) If several workstations are attached to the same host, it is wasteful of network resources to transmit multiple copies of data to the group of workstations.

Three distributed GKS implementations have been described in the literature, NOVA*GKS,[14] CNR GKS[2] and GOCS.[5] GOCS is briefly described here as a representative example.

The paper by Egelhaaf and Schürmann[5] describes a system which offers a distributed GKS in an open network. The system, GOCS – The GKS-Oriented Communication System, was developed for DFN which is the German research network connecting universities and research laboratories. The motivation for the project came from scenarios such as a physicist wanting to work interactively with a data analysis program running in another laboratory, or a scientist wanting to work interactively with a numerical program running on a supercomputer at another site, or cooperative working where a number of people at geographically distinct locations work together on, say, a CAD exercise.

DFN is a heterogeneous network with computers from many different manufacturers running many different operating systems. DFN at that time supported layers 1-4 of the OSI reference model and GOCS was based on the transport layer, T.70. The project designed a workstation interface, WSI, which is similar to that used by NOVA*GKS[14] and the CNR system.[2] It is a high level device independent interface.

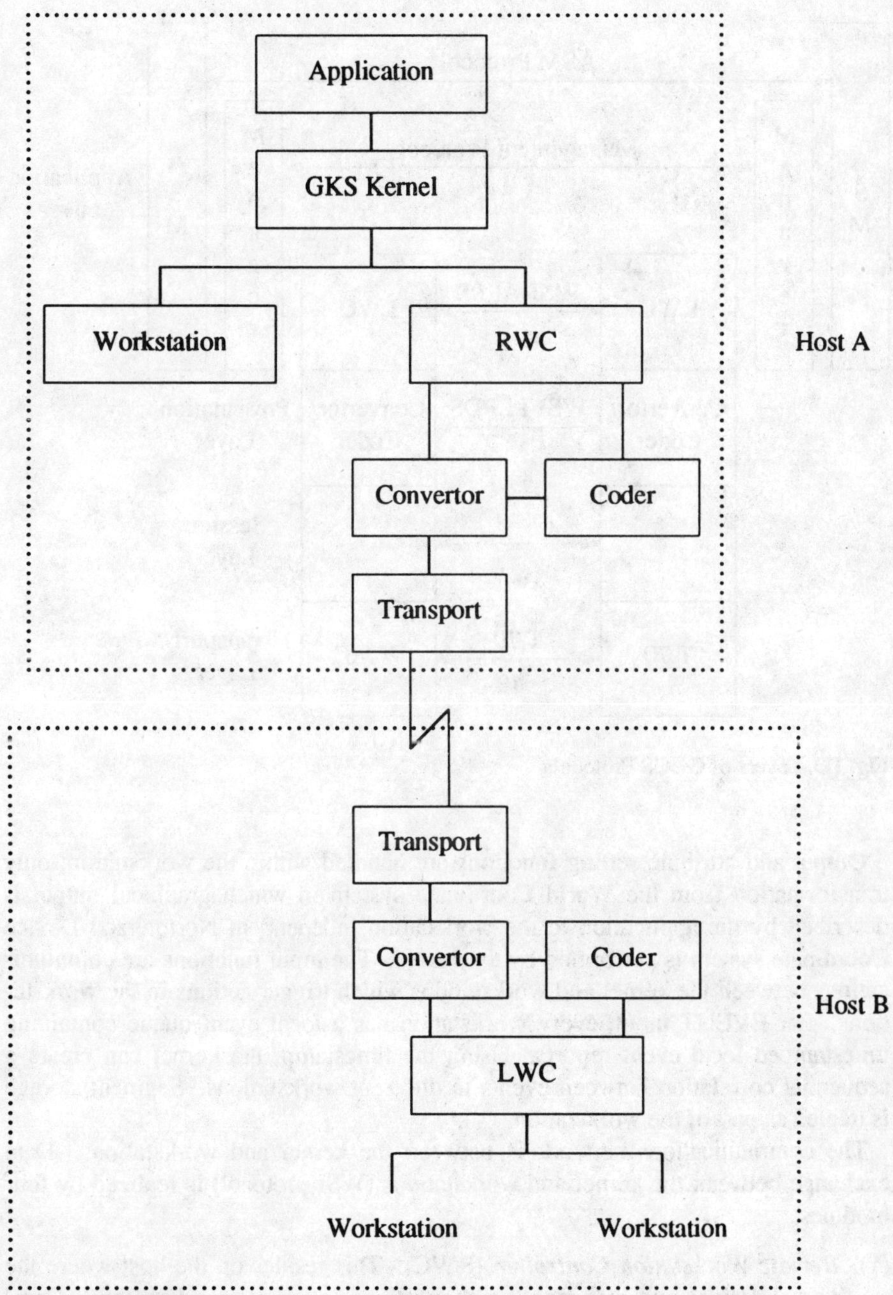

Fig. 1.2. GOCS Architecture

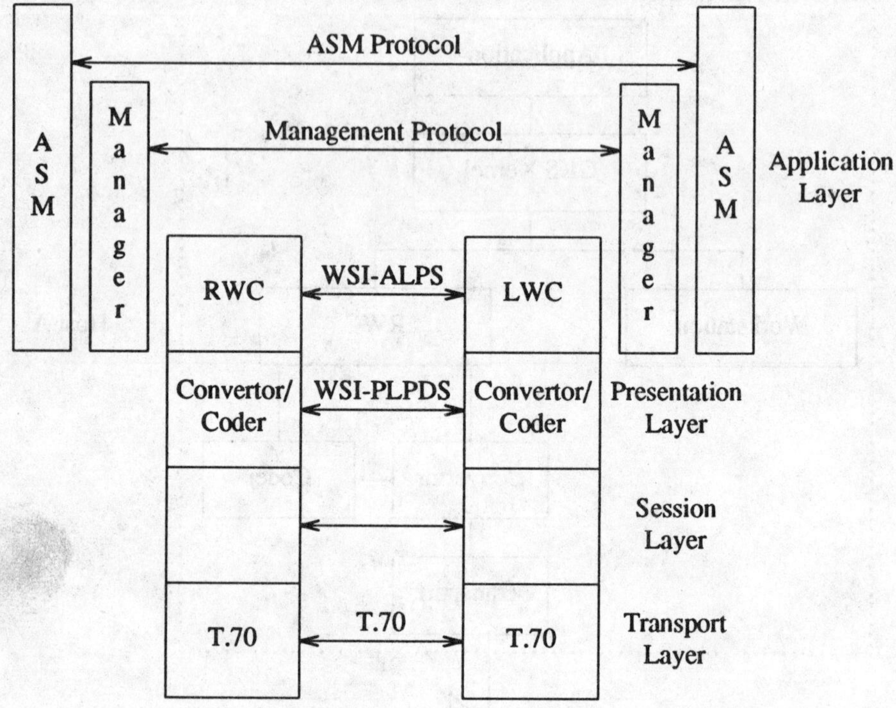

Fig. 1.3. Layers of GOCS Protocols

Output and attribute setting functions are handled within the workstation; only transformation from the World Coordinate system in which graphical output is described by the application to the workstation independent Normalized Device Coordinate system is performed by the kernel. The input functions are communications between the kernel and workstations which trigger actions in the workstations. For EVENT input, every workstation has a local event queue containing timestamped local event reports. Using the timestamp, the kernel can create a sequential correlation between events in different workstations. Segment storage is treated as part of the workstation.

The communications network is between the kernel and workstations. Data exchange between the kernel and workstations (WSI protocol) is realized by four modules:

(1) *Remote Workstation Controller* (RWC). This resides on the host where the kernel resides and manages the connections to remote workstations. Communication is through the WSI. It initiates the transfer of graphical information addressed to workstations on the remote host. If the information is

addressed to more than one workstation on the remote host, the data are only transported once.

(2) *Local Workstation Controller* (LWC). This resides on the workstation host and communicates with the RWC. It supervises the workstations and distributes WSI primitives to workstations.

(3) *Converter, Encoder and Decoder*. These entities convert the WSI data structures to protocol data units. Two encoding types are supported: a clear text encoding and a character encoding. The latter is much more compact. The clear text encoding is human-readable. The character encoding uses the principles defined for the Computer Graphics Metafile character encoding.

The GOCS architecture is shown in Fig. 1.2. GOCS provides facilities to start and control the running of applications in a remote host. This is done through an entity called *Applications Support and Management* (ASM). GOCS also provides a *Distributed GKS-Manager* (DGM) whose purpose is to ensure that GKS applications can run without change from local and remote workstations. It deals with issues such as addressing.

The GOCS protocols are structured in four layers as shown in Fig. 1.3. The ASM protocol allows start and control of applications. The Management protocol is the communication between DGM entities. The WSI presentation layer protocol data syntax (WSI-PLPDS) defines how graphical information in a common syntax and encoding is to be exchanged. The application layer protocol syntax (WSI-ALPS) defines the graphical information to be exchanged.

The Computer Graphics Metafile. The Computer Graphics Metafile (CGM) provides a means of storing two-dimensional static graphical information in a standardized way. By the end of 1987 over two dozen companies in the USA had released products or announced plans for products incorporating support for the CGM. Three kinds of product are emerging: applications such as CAD or business graphics packages may offer the ability to write a CGM file capturing one or more of the pictures created during a design session, second applications such as desktop publishing systems or printer spoolers which can read in CGM files and make some use of the pictures contained therein (for example paste into document or print on device), and third a small number of applications (such as graphics editors) can take in a CGM picture description, manipulate it and write it out again as a CGM description.

A major boost was given to CGM in the USA at the Integrate '88 demonstration at the NCGA '88 conference and exhibition held in Anaheim in March 1988.[10] Integrate '88 was a multivendor systems integration demonstration which incorporated four application areas typically found in a multifaceted corporation: engineering/ design, corporate communications/ financial analysis, graphics arts, and computer-aided publishing. Some 38 vendors took part in the demonstration. Multi-vendor equipment and software were linked together through an ethernet communications infrastructure running TCP/IP and used CGM as the standard picture interchange format. The demonstration was organized as a series of scenarios. In a typical scenario an operator would retrieve a design created on a

CAD program. The CAD representation was then modified and output as a file in CGM format. In this format it would then be sent to the graphics art department for enhancement or directly to printing and publishing for merging with text in a brochure. Similar procedures were be used to exchange files between finance, graphics arts, and printing and publishing. It was an impressive demonstration of the potential of interchange formats such as CGM in promoting product harmonization and is worth mentioning for that reason alone.

A similar demonstration was organized for the Eurographics UK Chapter Conference in Manchester in March 1989. Over 20 companies took part in this. Whereas Integrate'88 only used the MAP/TOP CGM profile, a subset of CALSA, the main technical achievement of the Manchester demonstration was that it involved the use of a less restrictive profile.

Events such as the above have demonstrated the need for CGMs to be exchanged over networks. The natural networking services for this are file transfer (for exchange of complete CGMs) and file access (for exchange of partial CGMs e.g. of selected pictures from a complete CGM).

The ARGOSI project has explored the mapping of CGM onto FTAM via a new Document Type, which defines a mapping of the CGM structure onto the FTAM 'virtual filestore'.

Windowing Systems. The last decade has seen a rapid growth in the use of windowing systems, both as a means of providing a highly interactive user interface on workstations and as a management framework for the display and manipulation of graphical information.

A Workshop in the UK in April 1985[8] reviewed the history of window systems (WS), attempted to define a methodology and considered the major unresolved issues at the time. At this time three major areas for discussion were identified:

(1) *Application interfaces*. At what level should the application interface be placed? Two extremes are the graphics system producing pixel changes in windows or being incorporated as part of the window system. Almost certainly the interface will be somewhere between these two extremes. Papers have appeared in the literature describing systems which have taken different approaches to the graphics system/ window system relationship. GAV[7] is an example of a window system built on top of GKS, whilst GKS* (ZGDV Darmstadt) is an example of a GKS implementation sitting on top of a window system. General consensus has been reached that the graphics system should sit on top of the window system.

(2) *Architectural model*. For efficiency, early WS tended to be part of the operating system kernel. The SUN Windows system (SunView) was the first attempt to put a large part of the WS in the user address space leaving only a small part in the UNIX kernel. This had the advantage that the code was much easier to debug but required clients to relink if changes were made to the WS. Also, unless inter-process communication is fast and efficient, the system cannot provide a good user interface. More recently systems have been built which define the WS as a process which can be accessed via

remote procedure calls. By keeping the protocol simple, it is possible for the WS to be implemented on a variety of devices. This has the major advantage that applications become portable and require no relinking to move from one display to another. Also, it provides distributed access to the system if the procedure call mechanism works across a network.

(3) *User interface.* Many of the existing systems appear the same on the surface but frequently have different philosophies once the surface is scratched. Some consistency in design principles, while still leaving the ability to do commercial tailoring, is essential.

The last few years has seen the X Window System[12] become established as the de facto standard windowing system for use on high performance workstations, and particularly for use where distribution of the windowing system across a network is required.

The first ten versions of the X Window System were developed as part of Project Athena at MIT. Version 11 (called X11)[11] was designed by a large set of people from a wider range of companies and was reviewed quite widely by others. Consequently, it was a more mature system than its predecessors and gained much wider acceptability in the community.

The Datastream Definition of X11 (i.e. the 'protocol') is currently undergoing standardization within ANSI, and may eventually be submitted for ISO/IEC standardization.

X11 divides a window system into a 'base window system' on which are built a 'window manager' which controls the size and placement of windows and an 'input manager' which controls input devices. Communication with the base window system is defined by a communications protocol using asynchronous stream-based inter-process communication.

The main feature of X11 is that it enables an application to use windows on any display in a network, in a device independent and network transparent manner. X11 is based on a *client/server* model. A client, or application, connects to a server via a network connection. Each display and associated input devices has an associated server. X11 regards the display as a scarce resource with a number of applications requiring to make use of its screen space. Consequently X11 defines the server as controlling the physical display and responsible for multiplexing client requests to the display, and demultiplexing input to appropriate clients. Several clients may have connections open to a server at one time. Similarly, a single client may have connections open to a number of different servers at the same time. All device dependencies are handled in the server so the application is device independent.

Clients and servers communicate over a reliable duplex byte stream with a simple block protocol on top. Within a machine, a local interprocess communication is used. Otherwise any convenient communications protocol that can provide a reliable duplex byte stream can be used.

X11 can be thought of as having three main components:

(1) X Server: which is very device specific (but a model implementation is provided with X11).
(2) X Protocol: which defines the connection between clients and servers.
(3) X Library: which, at the client end, interfaces the application, graphics system or high level parts of the WMS to the X Server using the X Protocol.

To simplify use of the X Library, there may also be:

(4) X Toolkit: which provides a higher level interface to X Library and handles initialization, defaults and overall style. Many different X Toolkits exist.

The structure of X11 is illustrated in Fig. 1.4.

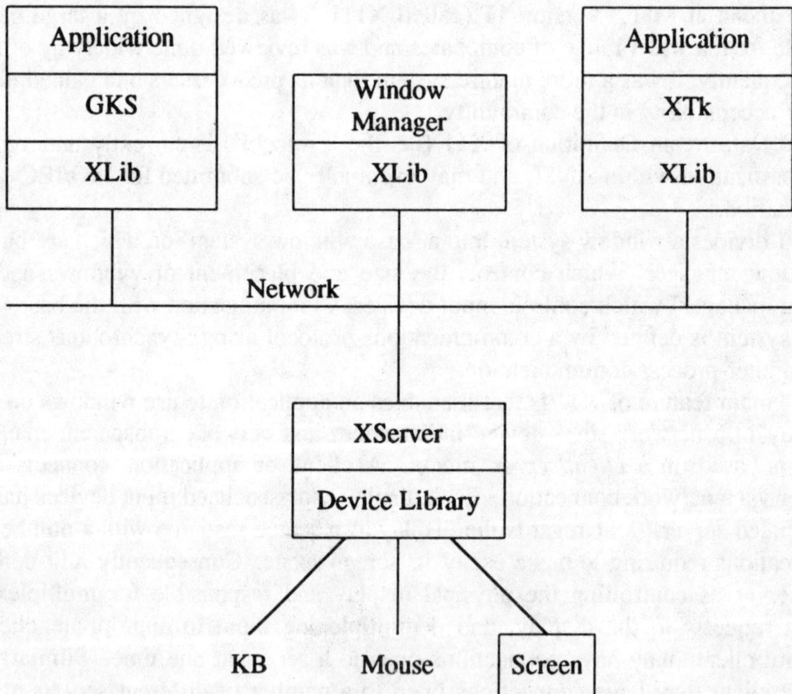

Fig. 1.4. X11 Architecture

A PEX extension to the X Library and X Server to support 3D viewing, rendering and the PHIGS structure store has been developed.[3, 13] As part of the effort to standardize X11 through ANSI and ISO/IEC, a mapping onto a full OSI stack has been developed (see Sect. 4.4).

References

1. D.B. Arnold and D.A. Duce (1990), *Computer Graphics Standards – The First Generation*, Butterworths.
2. R. Bettarini, G. Faconti, and L. Moltedo (1985), ''Extending GKS to a Distributed Architecture'', in *Proceedings of Eurographics 85*, ed. C.E. Vandoni: North-Holland.
3. W.H. Clifford, J.I. McConnell, and J.S. Salz (1988), ''The Development of PEX a 3D Graphics Extension to X11'', in *Proceedings of Eurographics 88*, ed. D.A. Duce and P. Jancene, North-Holland.
4. D.A. Duce and F.R.A. Hopgood (1987), ''The Graphical Kernel System (GKS)'', *Computer-Aided Design* **19**(8), pp.396-409.
5. C. Egelhaaf and G. Schürmann (1987), ''GOCS - The GKS-oriented Communications System'', in *Proceedings of Eurographics 87*, ed. G. Maréchal, North-Holland.
6. G. Enderle, K. Kansy, and G. Pfaff (1987), *Computer Graphics Programming: GKS - The Graphics Standard, 2nd Ed*, Springer-Verlag.
7. H.I.M Hartelt, L.P. Magalhaes, and B.M. Daltrini (1987), ''A Window Management System on Top of GKS'', in *Proceedings of Eurographics 87*, ed. G. Maréchal, North-Holland.
8. F.R.A. Hopgood, D.A. Duce, E.V.C. Fielding, K. Robinson, and A.S. Williams (Eds) (1985), *Methodology of Window Management*, EurographicSeminars, Springer-Verlag.
9. F.R.A. Hopgood, D.A. Duce, J.R. Gallop, and D.C. Sutcliffe (1986), *Introduction to the Graphical Kernel System (GKS), 2nd Ed*, Academic Press.
10. A.M. Mumford (1988), ''Integrating at NCGA'', *Computer Graphics Forum* **7**(3), pp.229-230.
11. R.W. Scheifler and J. Gettys (1986), ''The X Window System'', *Transactions on Graphics* **5**(2).
12. R.W. Scheifler, J. Gettys, and R. Newman (1988), *X Window System - C Library and Protocol Reference*, Digital Press.
13. S.W. Thomas (1991), ''PEX: Status, Directions and Alternatives?'', in *Distributed Window Systems Theory and Practice*, ed. D.B. Arnold, R.A. Day, D.A. Duce, J.R. Gallop, D.C. Sutcliffe, Eurographics Association, P.O. Box 16, CH-1288 Aire-la-Ville, Switzerland.
14. C.N. Waggoner, C. Tucker, and C.J. Nelson (1984), ''NOVA*GKS A Distributed Implementation of the Graphical Kernel System'', *Computer Graphics* **18**(3), pp.275-282.

2 Classification

2.1 Overview

2.1.1 Aims and Goals

There is a serious need to ensure that networking services provided by networking standards meet the requirements for the controlled transfer of graphical information generated by graphics standards and, furthermore, that both sets of standards meet the requirements of applications using graphics and networking. Furthermore, it is important that graphics, networking and applications communities communicate with each other to ensure the timely production of harmonized, relevant and useful standards.

The principal aim of the classification work was to investigate application requirements for graphics and networking services in combination and to present this information as a taxonomy of applications in terms of these requirements. The goals were:

(1) Classification of applications according to graphics requirements and the networking services needed for the graphics requirements.
(2) Matching requirements for combinations of graphics and networking services to the emerging family of ISO/IEC graphics and OSI standards.
(3) Identification of deficiencies in existing standards and identification of requirements for future standards in both graphics and networking.
(4) Provision of detailed information on the graphics and networking services necessary to implement a particular application and performance criteria for those services to be effective.
(5) Identification of services and performance requirements it is desirable to satisfy in the next generation of networks and standards in Europe.

When the project was defined, it was envisaged that the classification scheme would be based around the ideas of applications, application areas and classes of applications which share common service requirements. Service requirements would be described as combinations of graphics and networking services, for example, the ability to transfer 2D pictures between processes running in different host machines. A classification scheme is then achieved by identifying which applications belong to the class of applications associated with a particular set of service requirements.

To establish such a classification scheme, it is essential to derive an understanding of how current applications use combinations of graphics and networking services, together with an understanding of how requirements will evolve in the future. Requirements can never be totally divorced from the technology and so it is also necessary to have an understanding of how the underlying technology will evolve, leading to speculation on how existing applications can use improved technology and what new applications become possible because of improved performance and other characteristics.

In deriving the classification scheme, it became clear that a single set of application requirements could be met in a number of different ways, each resulting in a different use of graphics and networking services. For example, a distributed application might have two possible network links involving graphics at different stages in the application; different realizations of the application might use one or other or both of these links and the graphics and networking services required in each case would be different. It was decided that effort should be concentrated on studying and classifying the links according to the graphical information being transferred and the networking services required to transfer that graphical information.

2.1.2 Collection of the Data

Initially, information about applications was gained through a series of interviews. Visits were arranged to organizations developing applications which use graphics and networking, either now or will do in the future. Technical people in these organizations were interviewed by a team of up to three people from the project. In order to gain consistent information from interviews carried out by different members of the project, a questionnaire was constructed to guide the interviews. Although the information collected in this way was of high quality and gave a good insight into the use of graphics and networking in combination, it was expensive to collect both in terms of manpower and time.

Subsequently, an alternative approach was taken. A postal questionnaire was constructed, based on the questionnaire used to guide the interviews and on a set of possible classification metrics. The aim was to gather information from a broader spectrum of applications. The questionnaire was sent from the UK to approximately 2300 contacts, mainly in Europe and North America. Further mailings were carried out more locally by partners in other European countries (mainly in Italy, but also in France and Germany). 140 questionnaires were returned, but with a disappointing number from North America.

A summary of the results of the data collection is given in Sect. 2.2.

2.1.3 Relationship to External Activities

A study of user requirements for future computer graphics standards has been made under the auspices of ISO/IEC JTC1/SC24/WG1. The ARGOSI work differed from that in that the focus of attention in the ARGOSI work was specifically on the use of graphics over networks with particular reference to OSI.

A study of the requirements for networking between major sites in the Ile de France has been made by France Telecom.[1] This study discussed general networking applications and focussed on the bandwidth needs. The ARGOSI study concentrated on the architectural requirements of applications. A selection of the sites participating in the France Telecom study were contacted to see if they had information relevant to the ARGOSI study.

2.2 Results of Data Collection

The data obtained from the interviews and the postal questionnaire were of different sorts. The postal questionnaire being non-interactive, focused on simple multiple choice questions. Although interviews were also guided by a set of multiple choice questions, they also presented an opportunity to understand the architecture of the applications studied, which was important in producing the taxonomy. A selected subset of the interview data is presented later where examples of the taxonomy are given.

2.2.1 General

The postal questionnaire replies indicate that there is considerably less experience of applications that use graphics and networking than was envisaged when the postal survey was devised. It appears that there is an opportunity for guiding the appropriate standards, before the use of graphics over networks becomes widespread.

2.2.2 Graphics Used

Although 2D graphics is the most popular, the use of 3D is significant. There is some use of 4D in all application areas. The additional dimension could be time or 4D could be used in data space.

Most respondents seem to use more than one graphics standard. GKS is very widely used. Among 3D standards, there is relatively little usage of GKS-3D compared with PHIGS. This could either reflect or be reflected by the relative availability of products. CGM is widely used.

Where graphics standards are not used, this appeared to be due to insufficient functionality or insufficient performance. This may reflect that, historically, many users have written their own graphics software (often targeted at a specific device and its functionality and optimized for that device) and general purpose standards with their device-independence compare unfavourably with these optimized solutions.

The response for X11 was high, but it is unclear from the results whether Xlib or a toolkit is used by applications or whether X11 happens to be the workstation environment and whether Xlib graphics primitives are used. It is unclear from the responses the degree to which X11 is used as a distributed system or just on one workstation.

The responses showed some variation in picture complexity between application areas. The number of points defining fill area primitives is large in cartography and simulation and to some degree in graphics arts; cartographic applications show a large number of points per polyline. These results for cartography are confirmed by the interviews. Graphics standards at present do not impose on their implementations a requirement to handle high data volumes, which does not serve these applications well.

Data compression appears not to be widely considered at present. However interviews did reveal situations where data compression would be significantly used. It is also important to use the correct primitives. In existing commercial applications, it emerged from interviews that filled polygons are translated to (many) lines, resulting in the transmission of unnecessarily large data volumes; this is probably a legacy of pre-standard graphics software where fill area primitives could not be relied on to be present.

2.2.3 Networking Used

Many respondents are using DARPA protocols (including TCP/IP) and DECNET. More than half the people who answered the question about networking type have more than one network type. There is a strong peak in the results in LAN usage. The results concerning physical bandwidth appear to reflect the current usage of ethernet. Where networking standards are not used, this was due to a variety of reasons. These were chiefly insufficient performance, too much money, poor implementations, but the 'other' response was also represented highly. This may reflect that, for networking to take place, some agreement needs to exist between the two parties and so users' concerns are targeted at the cost and quality of the implementations of these agreements. There was clearly a different profile to the reasons why graphics standards were not used and the observations on each may provide insight.

2.3 A Taxonomy for Application Classification

2.3.1 Overview

The classification described below concentrates on the use of particular network associations that transfer graphical data between co-operating components of a distributed application, and classifies them according to the graphical information being transferred and the network services required to transfer that graphical information. A set of metrics, referred to as a taxonomy, has been defined to separate the different uses of network associations and to characterize those uses in terms of what graphical data are being transferred, how the data are being selected, how the transfer is being controlled and what quality of service is required in terms of quantity of data, rate of transfer, and acceptable errors. Note that for the purposes of classifying an application using this taxonomy it is assumed that the application can be decomposed into distinct distributed components each joined by one or more identifiable associations. If multiple associations are involved then each association is treated separately within the characterization of the application.

For the purpose of this taxonomy an 'association' is defined as a connection established between two components for the purpose of conducting a series of 'transactions'. The association may or may not be closed down at the end of this series of transactions, depending on the circumstances in effect. For example, the association may be kept permanently open, in some circumstances, or there might be a defined end-point to a series of transactions, after which the association is closed. Alternatively, there may be a more complex strategy involved in the setting up and closing down of associations.

This concept of an association has a similarity to the concept of an 'application association' described in the OSI Reference Model (ISO 7498), and in more detail in the OSI Association Control Service (ISO 8649). However, the two concepts should **not** be equated – as used in this taxonomy an association is intended to describe the most general type of network connection, be it a full OSI application association or one based on other networking models and protocols. At present, however, the taxonomy does regard an association as having a defined beginning and end (which would map onto association 'establishment' and 'release' in OSI terminology). The possibility of atomic (i.e. 'single shot') network transactions, with no concept of association establishment, is not catered for. This reflects the nature of the applications studied when deriving the taxonomy.

The taxonomy defines a 'control' metric to categorize the nature of the control of the series of transactions conducted over an association. This metric describes the behaviour of the 'application' with regard to the networking services it uses, and not that of the association itself. The taxonomy does not characterize the services provided by the underlying network – rather it characterizes the demands placed upon the network by the graphics component(s) of the application.

The metrics of the taxonomy are described in the following section. How these metrics were derived and why this set of metrics has been chosen is also described below (see Sect. 2.3.3). While the metrics themselves are likely to be stable, it is expected that the values of the metrics will be extended and areas where this may be anticipated are also described. The set of metrics form the basis of the taxonomy framework which is detailed further together with an initial elaboration of the framework.

2.3.2 Classification Metrics

The Semantic Content of Data Transferred Across the Network. This metric characterizes the kinds of graphics data that an application may require to be transferred across an association. The characterization used is an extended version of the ISO/IEC Reference Model for Computer Graphics (ISO/IEC 11072). The top two levels have been added to those of the reference model.

In order to understand the characterization, an outline of the Computer Graphics Reference Model (CGRM) is first given, at a coarse level of detail. The key idea in the CGRM is the notion of an 'environment'. To understand complex activities, there is a need to break them down into simpler activities which are easier to understand and describe. Each environment can be thought of as a set of data types and processes which completely describe computer graphics at a certain level of abstraction.

The CGRM consists of a hierarchy of five environments; the environments closer to the application have less knowledge of the hardware and more of the application and vice versa for the environments closer to the operator. Although the number of environments is to some extent arbitrary, the choice of levels was guided by the need for simplicity of description and the need to distinguish different levels of abstraction in the handling of data. The levels of abstraction chosen in the CGRM are based on those that are present (or in some cases should have been present!) in the first generation of computer graphics standards. Each level of abstraction corresponds to a well-defined state of the graphical information, a state in which it would make sense to store and retrieve graphical information.

A simplified representation of an environment is shown in Fig. 2.1. An environment has a single interface for incoming data from the immediately higher environment for graphical output information and a single interface for incoming data from the immediately lower environment for graphical input information. Graphical output information may be distributed to more than one instance of an environment at the next lower level; and graphical input information may be distributed to more than one instance of an environment at the next higher level.

The rectangular boxes within an environment are processes which in the case of output information ('graphical output transformer') transforms the output information received from the next higher level into the appropriate data at the level of abstraction of the environment, and in the case of input information ('graphical

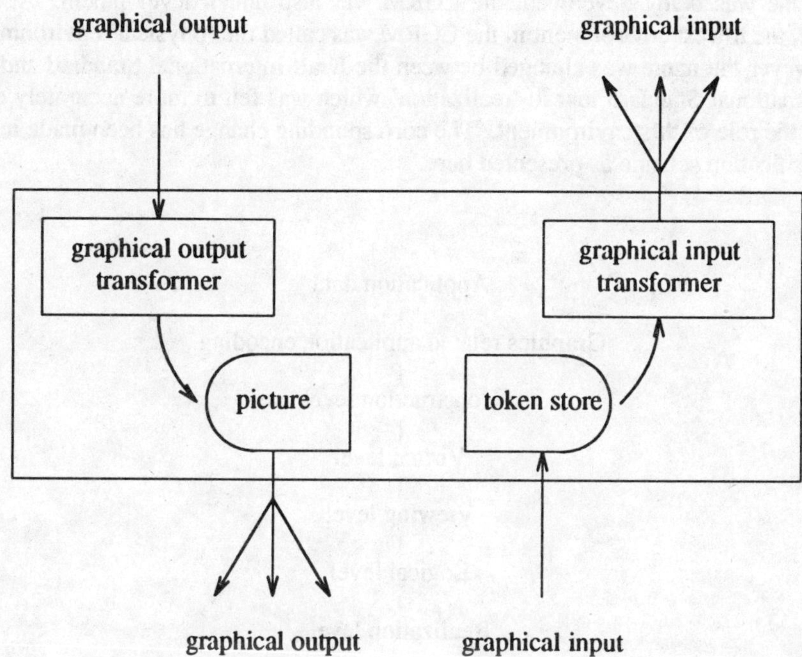

Fig. 2.1. A Simplified CGRM Environment

input transformer') transforms the input information from this level of abstraction into the form required by the next higher environment level.

The 'picture' and 'token store' are stores for graphical output and input information, respectively. The generic name 'picture' is meant to capture the idea of the picture that the application is striving to create at each level of abstraction. The 'token store' captures the idea of constructing application level input values from tokens generated at lower levels, initially as a result of external (operator, operating system, etc.) actions.

The CGRM per se provides a more detailed internal model for an environment, in order to describe the relationship between input and output in more detail, and also the mechanism by which graphical output and input information may be constructed within an environment. However, since only the levels of abstraction are important for the semantic content metric, it is not necessary to go into a more detailed discussion of the CGRM.

The characterization of semantic content used here is based on the five levels identified in the CGRM, plus two additional levels, 'application data' and 'graphics related application encoding' (see Fig. 2.2). Whilst the ARGOSI classification scheme was being developed, the CGRM was also under development. At that time, the lowest environment in the CGRM was called the 'physical' environment. However the name was changed between the Draft International Standard and the International Standard text to 'realization' which was felt to more accurately capture the role of this environment. The corresponding change has been made in the classification scheme as presented here.

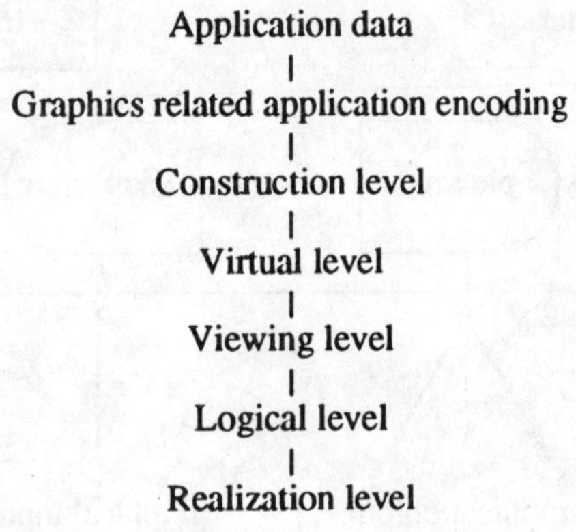

Fig. 2.2. Semantic Content

'Application data' is the highest level of abstraction in the model and characterizes data which have no direct graphical presentation. An example would be a spreadsheet. Although the values of particular collections of cells in a spreadsheet might be represented as a graphical chart, the spreadsheet itself (including the formulae relating cells) has no such intrinsic presentation. The taxonomy does not discuss any substructure within application data and groups all such data under one heading. If particular standards for application data transfer were to be discussed, the application data value of the semantic content metric would need to be refined further.

'Graphics related application encoding' refers to data that is in some way graphics related, but does not contain graphical information which could be directly executed to produce an image. For example, product data e.g. STEP, and business graphics pie charts, etc., could be considered in this category.

Data at the 'construction level' is constructed from graphics related application data and represents a model from which specific graphics scenes can be produced. Input is related to the construction level model and represented in a precise form required by the application.

At the 'virtual' level the scene of the model to be viewed is constructed and the graphics data represents this scene in terms of a set of virtual output primitives. The geometry of these output primitives should be completely defined so that scenes are geometrically complete. (However, this is not strictly true for the current set of ISO graphics standards.) Input received at the virtual level will be in the coordinate system of the scene and have properties which may be used to distinguish components of the scene.

The 'viewing' level takes a specific view of the scene producing the picture to be displayed. Output primitives in the viewing environment may have a lower dimensionality than in the virtual environment. The viewing level relates input received to specific pictures being viewed.

The 'logical' level renders the picture as an image ready for presentation. The image may still be considered to be consisting of a set of logical output primitives, however all attributes which determine the visual appearance of the primitives have been bound at this level. The logical level accumulates input from the realization level, there does not need to be a one-to-one correspondence between the input data received at these levels.

The 'realization' level presents the image for display to a specific device. The data representing the picture at this level could be device dependent, for example device opcodes/ pixels/ colours. Input at this level has been received directly from the input device.

The semantic content metric does not characterize any particular presentation technique as such, it simply addresses from a graphics structuring aspect, the levels of abstraction of the data to which access is required. The values of this metric are: (APPLICATION-DATA, GRAPHICS-RELATED, CONSTRUCTION, VIRTUAL, VIEWING, LOGICAL, REALIZATION). The semantic level determines the processing that needs to take place in the receiving end of the graphical data. It also determines what manipulations are possible in the receiving end, without requiring additional data to be received. To take a simple case, if data at the virtual level is transmitted, the view can be changed in the receiver. If data are transmitted at the logical level, the receiver in general cannot display a view without receiving more data.

An individual association can only transfer data at one semantic level. Many applications will appear to transfer data at different semantic levels across the same association, for example combined image and contour data. Closer inspection shows that in most of these cases, the data are actually at the same semantic level, because a common semantic level is necessary in order to compose the data.

An application may transfer data at different semantic levels across the same network. These cases are described by multiple associations.

Dimensionality. This metric gives an indication of the dimensionality of graphics data transferred across the network. Dimensionality in general covers a number of different kinds of entities:

(1) Euclidean geometric dimension of the graphics data;
(2) Non-Euclidean geometric dimension of the graphic data (for example, data in a projective space expressed using homogeneous coordinates);
(3) Time;
(4) Combined geometric and data space dimensionality. For example, in PHIGS PLUS, primitives can be specified with data; essentially the control points defining the data are points in a higher dimensional space in which some of the dimensions define the geometry of the primitive and others define associated data which may be used to determine the colours of points in the primitive.

For the present classification scheme, a limited range of values is considered for this metric (2D, 3D, 4D, HIGHER) with meanings:

2D 2 Euclidean dimensions,
3D 3 Euclidean dimensions,
4D 3 Euclidean dimensions plus time,
HIGHER 4 Projective dimensions, plus time and data space dimensions.

Data Source. This metric indicates whether the data to be accessed are a complete, known body, of structured information (such as a complete file of stored information), or whether it is an individual primitive or token, or group of primitives or tokens that is being generated to interact with or construct a picture. The values of the metric are (COMPLETE, PARTIAL).

Control. The control metric indicates which of the ends of the association has control over the selection of data and initiation of transactions conducted over the association. It also characterizes the direction of data flow in relation to the initiator. The values of the metric and their meanings are described in Table 2.1. The components connected by an association are labelled A and B.

Table 2.1. The Control Metric

Control	Initiator	Dataflow Direction Support	Selection Support	Disposition
GIVE-ME	A	towards A	B	A
TAKE-THIS	A	towards B	A	B
TWO-WAY	A or B	towards A or towards B	B or A	A or B

For the GIVE-ME and TAKE-THIS styles of control, the initiator of each transaction is the same throughout the sequence of transactions conducted over the association. For the TWO-WAY style of control, the initiative for each transaction may pass freely between the components involved.

The data flow direction column indicates the direction in which the data selected by each transaction will flow. A GIVE-ME transaction initiated by A requests B to send some information. The data flow direction is thus towards A. For TAKE-THIS, A is providing information to B and thus the flow is towards B. For TWO-WAY, the flow may vary between transactions.

The selection support column indicates which of the components is responsible for selecting the data to be transferred, from the data source.

The disposition support column indicates which of the components is responsible for disposing of the data transferred from the data source.

Selection Criteria. The selection of information, whether stored locally or remotely, is another important metric which is used here to classify applications. This metric takes three values, namely WHOLE, STATIC-SUBSET and DYNAMIC-SUBSET.

Although these values are primarily motivated by the bottom five semantic levels, the concept of selection is a more general one which applies equally to graphics related application encoding and to the application data levels.

- WHOLE: refers to the selection of the whole data structure rather than some subpart of it. Knowledge of the internal structure is not required. For example, selecting a whole file of CGMs.
- STATIC-SUBSET: refers to the selection of information based on criteria directly related to the predetermined structure to the organization of the stored data. As an example, consider a collection of graphics data structured according to a number of application-defined grid squares (each with a unique number). Selecting grid square '19' is a STATIC-SUBSET selection of that grid square's contents, even though the actual graphical content may vary over time. The selection is directly related to the organization of the data; no transformation of the selection criterion is necessary.
- DYNAMIC-SUBSET: refers to the selection of information based on criteria which need not bear a direct relationship to the structure or organization of the stored information. Geometric selection criteria would involve the selection of graphical information through satisfying some geometric relationship. Examples are, select all graphical information contained within a given window (geometric region), or select all graphic surface primitives for which the z-coordinate of the surface normal in normalized projection coordinates is greater than zero (i.e. back face cull – select front faces). Attribute selection criteria would involve the selection of graphical information based on non-geometric attributes. (These are not limited to those attributes defined in the current family of graphics standards.) For example, select all 'green' graphic primitives.

Quality of Service. The metrics defined so far distinguish applications in fundamental ways. It is likely that the applications falling within different boxes would be satisfied by different standards. Quality of Service here refers to all the parameters in the classification which describe how the graphics over OSI service scales up or down. The same set of standards is likely to be used, but the execution of the service request may take longer (to perhaps an unacceptable degree) or be error-prone.

- DATA VOLUME. This describes how much graphics data is transferred in a single transaction. However, the measurement is in terms of target data and not in terms of number of octets transferred. Data compression for the purposes of reducing the volume of transmitted data is regarded as internal to the transaction transferring the data. The data volume should probably be expressed in terms which depend on the semantic content of the data transferred. However for the classification scheme employed here, data volume is expressed as a pair of values ('total number of coordinates plus total number of cells', 'number of primitives in a picture'). Note that this assumes, in terms of size, approximately a one-to-one correspondence between a coordinate and a colour value, which may or may not be correct. Each value is expressed as an order of magnitude. Note also that the x, y coordinates of a 2D-point count as two coordinates, not one. Similarly a 3D-point has 3 coordinates. Individual data values associated with graphical information are counted as additional coordinate values.
- TRANSACTION TIME. This metric is the minimum time for a single user interaction. This is measured from the user request leaving the user's local system to the completion of the response to the user. Units for transaction time are (FRAME RATE, SECONDS, MINUTES, HOURS, DAYS, LONGER).
- TRANSACTION INTERVAL. This metric is concerned with the frequency of transaction to one or more kinds of data being transferred from a remote machine. The metric provides a set of values indicating how frequently such transactions occur, as follows (FRAME RATE, SECONDS, MINUTES, HOURS, DAYS, LONGER).
- ACCEPTABLE ERROR RATE In principle it is possible for the user of a network to specify a maximum acceptable error rate for the task in hand. (For example, it is permitted in an OSI network for the user of the Session or Transport Services to specify an acceptable 'medium error rate' as part of the 'Quality of Service' required.) In this taxonomy this concept is represented as an 'acceptable error rate' which can take one of the values (NO-ERRORS, SPECIFIED-ACCEPTABLE, DONT-BOTHER).

  - NO-ERRORS indicates a value of 0 for acceptable error rate,
  - SPECIFIED-ACCEPTABLE indicates some known value,

– DONT-BOTHER indicates that the application is not critically dependent on a particular error rate – for example, there is more data following.

2.3.3 Derivation of Taxonomy

This section discusses the thinking behind the choice of the particular set of metrics described in the previous section. The purpose of the classification is to characterize applications according to their graphics and networking requirements, in essence according to their requirements for transferring graphical information. The strategy chosen to achieve this was to define a number of metrics, which would quantify these requirements and enable applications to be divided into groups according to the values of these metrics, i.e. the metrics would form a taxonomy. Thus, the metrics that were defined should enable applications with similar graphics and networking requirements to be grouped together and applications with differing requirements to be separated. The overall aim was that each group of applications would have a set of requirements that could be met by one standard or collection of standards. Different groups of applications would need different collections of standards. The metrics were chosen to reflect this, so that metrics, which were perceived as useful measures but would not alter the standard to be used, were grouped together.

During the development of the taxonomy, consideration was given to a number of metrics. Initially, attempts were made to classify whole applications and so metrics such as 'semantic content of graphics data used locally' and 'semantic content of data transferred across the network' were included. It soon became clear that classifying whole applications was very complex and that the graphics data existed at different levels at different stages of an application. In this case, the metric 'semantic content of graphics data used locally' possessed a set of values rather than a single value. In considering the transfer of data, the same application could have associations in different places according to the particular circumstances in which it was running; the metric 'semantic content of data transferred across the network' then either took alternative values or a set of values. Trying to interpret metrics each with a set of values was a very difficult task.

It was decided that better progress would be made if the classifications were based on associations rather than whole applications. The metric 'semantic content of data transferred across the network' was clearly necessary. Consideration was given to a metric concerned with the semantic content of data at the ends of the association as an alternative to the data 'used locally'. However, similar problems arose with it being a set of values and different approaches were adopted to characterize the ends of the association.

Another area of early discussion centred on how data was selected for transfer and where that selection was taking place, either before or after transfer. Following the idea of classifying single associations, accessing graphical data stored in a metafile at one end of an association was used as an example for this discussion. With the instigator of the transfer at the opposite end of the association to the data, either all or part of the metafile might be required. If part of the metafile was required, the whole of the metafile could be transferred and the selection made by the instigator or a part of the metafile could be selected and then transferred. The former is conceptually simple and allows the instigator the generality of selection but could be making very inefficient use of the network. The latter is more complex and means the network services must make the selection but would make more efficient use of the network. The standards required in each case would be clearly related but greater control would be needed in the latter case and so the metrics chosen need to distinguish between them. If, however, the instigator is at the same end of the association as the data, there is little difference in complexity between the two alternatives and the same standards might be able to be used.

To encapsulate these distinctions, the metrics 'selection criteria' (what data is required) and 'control' (which end controls the transfer) were defined. Discussion revealed that possible solutions included the whole file (possibly containing several metafiles), a single metafile, a single picture within a metafile, a single picture element (segment) within a picture or a part of the picture defined by some other means (e.g. a particular region, primitives with a particular attribute). These selections can be categorized as: everything, a part of the file defined within the structure of the file, and a part of the file defined in an independent manner. This led to the values WHOLE, STATIC-SUBSET and DYNAMIC-SUBSET for the selection criterion metric. The control metric was given the values GIVE-ME and TAKE-THIS to denote the relationship between the instigator and the data.

From this basis the discussion widened to consider interactive applications. These included both multiple transactions with a stored data file and interactions with a running process producing graphics. At one level, each atomic action could be classified as GIVE-ME or TAKE-THIS but this was considered to be a too low-level approach. Within a sequence of transactions there was a predominant method of control and it was this that was needed to be described by the metric. By adding the value TWO-WAY to the control metric, it was felt that this could be achieved. However, it was discovered that the selection criterion seemed to relate more to stored data than data being generated by a process. On reflection, the true distinction was found to be between a set of data that was complete and a set of data that was not complete (or still being generated). A new metric was defined to describe the state of the data, called the 'data source' and was given the values COMPLETE and PARTIAL.

Other discussion related to how remote execution and remote computation should be characterized. Remote job entry (RJE) could be viewed as GIVE-ME, in that the initiator requires the result of a certain computation. Alternatively, it could be viewed as TAKE-THIS, meaning the data defining the computation to be performed, followed by a GIVE-ME to return the results. A third alternative is that it is viewed as two separate associations i.e. one with TAKE-THIS control from RJE client to server, followed by a later TAKE-THIS control from server to client. Remote procedure call (RPC) can also be viewed as a GIVE-ME, where the initiator is requiring a selection of the data (defined by the RPC parameters) from a PARTIAL data source (remote computation). There is also the possibility of separate associations within the RPC paradigm (e.g. 'callback' RPC). This is also an area for further study.

Dimensionality of the data being transferred was included from the outset as a metric. The current values are 2D, 3D, 4D, and HIGHER. However, it has been realized that what the dimensions represent may be significant. For example, it may be necessary to distinguish between three Cartesian coordinates plus time and four dimensional homogeneous coordinates. This is a topic for further study.

Data volumes, transfer times and acceptable error rates are also important factors. Much data about these was collected in the postal questionnaire. While some of these items were initially included as metrics, since OSI services are scaleable depending upon the requirements, the same set of standards should be able to be used for both small and large quantities of data. If the data volume and transfer time require a certain transfer rate, then the network bandwidth must be increased to provide this without affecting the services provided. Consequently, a quality of service metric was introduced. The components of the quality of service metric should place requirements on the performance of the services provided, rather than on what services are provided. The components of the quality of service metric are DATA VOLUME, TRANSACTION TIME, TRANSACTION INTERVAL, and ACCEPTABLE ERROR RATE. Their values are orders of magnitude rather than precise values. Image compression was considered as a possible component since it too relates to the performance of the services. However, compression was considered to be part of the underlying services and an alternative to increasing the bandwidth. Conversely, some compression strategies discard some of the data, which is unacceptable in some circumstances, and so cannot be left to the services. Consideration was given to an image fidelity component to record whether discarding data was acceptable but this was left as a topic for further study.

Analysis of the data gained in interviews also suggested that geographical area might be an important aspect of the quality of service, but this again was left for further study.

Grouping these components together produced the realization that some of the initial metrics were not required. For example, the postal questionnaire and interviews had asked questions about animation, as this was considered to be important, and animation was included in the initial metrics. However, animation can be represented by equal values of transaction time and transaction interval and real-time animation by both of these having the value FRAME RATE and so animation does not feature in the final set of metrics. Data security, on the other hand, was considered to be independent of the types of graphics data being transferred and so was omitted as a component of quality of service.

It can be seen that the final set of metrics comprising the taxonomy is the result of several iterations involving the definition of metrics, gradual refinement of these metrics (including combination and omission of metrics proposed for the data collection phase of the work), and introduction of other metrics where this was found to be necessary. The final set of metrics is considered to be sufficient to characterize the associations between components of a distributed application.

The results obtained from the interviews carried out in the early stages of the work played an important part in the derivation of these metrics. The interviews concentrated on specific applications, whereas the postal questionnaire gave a broader summary across applications, and consequently more architectural information on the applications was obtained from the interviews. This observation was put to use to define the set of questions used to gain further information to substantiate the classification scheme in the final phase of the work.

2.3.4 Taxonomy Framework

A number of metrics that have been defined to characterize applications were described in Sect. 2.3.2. For the purposes of deriving the taxonomy, each metric has a small number of possible values, even if this means dividing the possible values into a number of ranges. A zero, nonexistent, or not-applicable value is included in the permissible values for each metric as appropriate.

The metrics, thus defined, can be envisaged as representing the axes of an n-dimensional grid of n-dimensional boxes. This n-dimensional grid is referred to as the taxonomy framework. A particular association can be inserted into one of the boxes by deriving the values of all the metrics and determining the appropriate box. That association has then been classified according to the scheme.

If the selection of metrics has been successful, then all the associations within a particular box will be satisfied by the same set of graphics and OSI services. Certain of the associations will be elaborated in this manner later in this chapter.

2.3.5 Initial Elaboration of the Taxonomy Framework

The taxonomy framework was described in the previous section. Understanding such an n-dimensional framework is a complex task. In this section, an attempt is made to provide such an understanding. The framework, based on the metrics described in Sect. 2.3.2, consists of 504 boxes, if the quality of service metric is omitted. It is not sensible to describe all these boxes. Instead, the framework is explored by taking a structured route through the framework, to illustrate what certain boxes represent, to indicate how their requirements might be met, and to see the changes that occur by moving to neighbouring boxes.

The boxes are denoted by the set of values of the metrics in the order in which they appear in Sect. 2.3.2, namely semantic content of data transferred across the network, dimensionality, data source, control and selection criterion. The starting point for the exploration is the box VIRTUAL, 2D, COMPLETE, GIVE-ME, WHOLE.

VIRTUAL, 2D, COMPLETE, GIVE-ME, WHOLE

The user requests that a whole file of 2D virtual graphics data be brought to the local node. The local node has control over viewing and the representation of attributes that determine the visual appearance of the graphics data.

For example, a user on a workstation requests a stored contour map be brought to the workstation. The contour map may be locally zoomed to allow the user to inspect selected detail.

Possible standards: CGM, FTAM.

If not all the information is required, then a different selection criterion may be used.

VIRTUAL, 2D, COMPLETE, GIVE-ME, STATIC-SUBSET

The user requests that a subset of a file, selected by a mechanism related to its storage structure, of 2D virtual graphics data be brought to the local node. The local node has control over viewing and the representation of attributes that determine the visual appearance of the graphics data.

For example, a user on a workstation may request a selected subset from a large number of stored contour maps.

Possible standards: CGM, FTAM (using the CGM Document Type).

VIRTUAL, 2D, COMPLETE, GIVE-ME, DYNAMIC-SUBSET

The user requests that a subset of a file of 2D virtual graphics data be brought to the local node. The selection is dynamic, i.e. is specified at the time of the request and is not related to the storage structure of the remote file.

For example, a user on a workstation may request a selected region from a large, complex picture archive or a centrally updated picture store. An example of this is a detailed map or a complex engineering drawing. Transmitting only the required region can have a considerable beneficial effect on the bandwidth requirement.

Possible standards: CGM, FTAM (using the CGM Document Type – see Sect. 4.2). There is no standard for making the dynamic selection.

Returning to the starting point, the user may be in the same location as the data and wishes to send the data elsewhere, leading to:

VIRTUAL, 2D, COMPLETE, TAKE-THIS, WHOLE

The user requests that a whole file of 2D virtual graphics data be sent to a remote node. That remote node then has control over viewing and the representation of attributes that determine the visual appearance of the graphics data.

For example, a user on a mainframe requests a stored contour map be sent to a workstation, where, for example, the contour map could be zoomed to allow inspection of selected detail or, alternatively, the contour could be plotted directly on a plotter.

Possible standards: CGM, FTAM or possibly CGM, Messaging Standard.

Changing the control again leads to:

VIRTUAL, 2D, COMPLETE, TWO-WAY, WHOLE

This box is more difficult to describe. It could involve the use of distributed graphics databases and distributed updating or it may even be an empty box. This is an example where more work is required.

The use of TWO-WAY as a control may be better seen by returning to the starting box and changing the data source to PARTIAL as well as the control to TWO-WAY.

VIRTUAL, 2D, PARTIAL, TWO-WAY, WHOLE

The user at a local node wishes to interact graphically with a process running on a remote node. The user wishes to see the current state of the 2D picture and, on the basis of what he sees, to indicate graphically changes he wishes to be made to the picture. In response to the changes, an updated picture is sent to the local node for display. Other similar scenarios will fall into this box.

For example, a user at a workstation is running a route finding program on a mainframe. When the route is displayed on the workstation, the user wishes the route to go via a particular point and to avoid another point. This information is relayed to the mainframe, where the program generates a new route.

Possible standards: CGI, Terminal Management Standards.

Returning again to the starting point, the user may wish to deal with higher dimensional data than 2D. Thus:

VIRTUAL, 3D, COMPLETE, GIVE-ME, WHOLE

The user requests that a whole file of 3D virtual graphics data be brought to the local node. The local node has control over 3D viewing and the representation of attributes that determine the visual appearance of the graphics data.

For example, a user on a workstation requests a stored 3D scene be brought to the workstation. The internal relationships in the scene are bound but a local 3D walk-through is possible.

Possible standards: CGM (with 3D extensions), FTAM.

and higher again:

VIRTUAL, 4D, COMPLETE, GIVE-ME, WHOLE

The user requests that a whole file of 4D virtual graphics data be brought to the local node. The local node has control over viewing and the representation of attributes that determine the visual appearance of the graphics data.

An example depends upon the precise nature of the 4D data and more work is required in this area.

Possible standards: no graphics standards yet exist but FTAM could still be used for the transfer.

The final value, HIGHER, in this direction recognizes that data with greater dimensionality exist and need to be considered.

The final axis to be explored from the starting point is the semantic content of the data transferred across the network. Boxes along this axis indicate how much processing the data have undergone, where the data are in the pipeline, and what further processing may sensibly take place. The starting point has already been described and so the rest of the axis will be explored by examining the extremes, relative to the starting point.

APPLICATION-DATA, 2D, COMPLETE, GIVE-ME, WHOLE

The user requests that a whole file of application data be brought to the local node. The local node has control over all operations appropriate to the data being transferred.

For example, a user on a workstation requests a spreadsheet file be brought to the workstation. Any suitable package that accepts the spreadsheet data may be run on the workstation.

Possible standards: any appropriate application standard, FTAM.

At the other extreme:

REALIZATION, 2D, COMPLETE, GIVE-ME, WHOLE

The user requests that a whole file of realization-level data be brought to the local node. The local node may not manipulate the data in any way but may display it.

For example, a user on a workstation requests a screen dump be brought to the workstation from another workstation for display.

Possible standards: no formal standard exists for realization-level data but FTAM could still be used for the transfer.

2.4 Examples of Using the Taxonomy Framework

A number of examples of using the taxonomy framework are presented in this section. In Sect. 2.4.1, the examples show that the taxonomy framework can capture different graphics and networking requirements in its different boxes. In Sect. 2.4.2, the examples show that similar requirements are captured by a single box in the taxonomy framework. Sect. 2.4.3 describes different applications that use multiple associations. The question of the semantic content of image data is examined, in relation to its use, in Sect. 2.4.4. During the course of the work, it was realized that the taxonomy framework could be used as a design aid by examining the resource implications associated with different designs which fitted into different boxes. This is described in Sect. 2.4.5.

The applications that are discussed are drawn from the interviews carried out during the course of the work.

2.4.1 Wide Range of Requirements

Tables 2.2a and 2.2b show the classification of several different applications, leading to different boxes being used in the taxonomy framework.

2.4.2 Similar Requirements

In this section, a number of applications are presented which fall into the same box in the taxonomy framework. This box is denoted by:

Semantic content	VIRTUAL
Dimensionality	2D
Data source	COMPLETE
Control	GIVE-ME
Selection criterion	STATIC-SUBSET

Table 2.2a. Classification of applications

	Applications		
Metrics	UK met. pred. region[1]	Applic. prototype[2]	UK met. not pred. region[3]
Semantic Content	VIRTUAL	VIRTUAL	VIRTUAL
Dimension-ality	2D	2D	2D
Data Source	COMPLETE	COMPLETE	COMPLETE
Control	GIVE-ME	GIVE-ME	GIVE-ME
Selection Criteria	WHOLE	STATIC-SUBSET	DYNAMIC-SUBSET
Quality of Service:			
Data Volume	$(10^{4+},10^{1})$	$(10^{3+},10^{2})$	$(10^{4+},10^{1})$
Transaction Time	MINUTES	SECONDS	MINUTES
Transaction Interval	DAYS	MINUTES	DAYS
Error Rate	NO-ERRORS	NO-ERRORS	NO-ERRORS
Comments	large volume	complete, static back-ground	large volume
Application area	Meteorology / Cartography	Traffic information	Meteorology / Cartography

Notes

(1) Application 1 is from the UK Meteorological Office. The meteorologist requests a contour map for inspection at a local workstation. The regions of interest are predefined.

(2) Application 2 is the ARGOSI demonstrator (see Chap. 5). There is a static background and other local graphics needs to be merged with the transmitted picture.

(3) Application 3 is like application 1, except that the region requested need not be a predefined one.

In a number of cases, the application was still at the design stage at the time of the interviews. In these cases, the application could be placed in different boxes depending upon the design decisions; these alternative boxes are identified together with the design alternatives that led to their use.

Table 2.2b. Classification of applications

Metrics	Applications		
	Thomson Ocean Traffic[4]	RAL remote pic. lib.[5] Overview	One pic.
Semantic Content	CONSTRUCTION or VIRTUAL	REALIZATION	VIRTUAL
Dimension-ality	2D	2D	2D
Data Source	PARTIAL	COMPLETE	COMPLETE
Control	TAKE-THIS or GIVE-ME	GIVE-ME	GIVE-ME
Selection Criteria	WHOLE	STATIC-SUBSET	STATIC-SUBSET
Quality of Service:			
Data Volume	$(10^{2+},10^{0})$	$(10^{6},10^{0})$	$(10^{4},10^{2})$
Transaction Time	MINUTES	SECONDS	SECONDS
Transaction Interval	MINUTES	MINUTES	SECONDS
Error Rate	NO-ERRORS	DONT-BOTHER	NO-ERRORS
Comments	static background		
Application area	Traffic control / information	Education	Education

Notes

(4) Application 4 is an ocean traffic control application arising from an interview conducted by Thomson. A ship can display the tracks of all ships in the region under control. There are a number of design alternatives which lead to different values of the metrics. There is a static background.

(5) Application 5 arises from the coordination of graphics in the UK academic community. One specific problem is the provision of a network-accessible picture library. It should be possible to request a few specific pictures. It should also be possible to request that all pictures in a library be displayed as one image. For this complete image there is a design issue concerned with whether it is preferable to construct the image remotely and only transfer the remote image.

Distance Learning. In a proposed distance learning project (Italy), the box denoted the set of values of the metrics corresponding to a situation where a student initiates the transfer of graphical information to the student's workstation. If instead, part of the distance learning application is executed at the student's workstation, the semantic content is APPLICATION-DATA. If the course-ware centre initiated the transfer, the session control metric is TAKE-THIS.

Manufacturing. In a manufacturing application under design in the UK, the operator carries out a wiring task, guided by a picture transmitted from a central location. The operator requests a picture when ready for the next task. The selection criterion could be regarded as WHOLE – the whole of the graphics information for the task is delivered; or the term WHOLE might correspond to a set of operating tasks, in which case the picture for a single task would correspond to STATIC-SUBSET.

Power Station CAD. This application in France involves the enquiry of a large CAD database over a wide (national) area. The user initiates the inquiry of the database. The semantic level depends on the degree of manipulation required in the user workstation. It is anticipated that the next version will use CGM. If the database consists of graphical information, it is likely that the data source metric would be COMPLETE. If on the other hand, the database contains application-oriented information but the network transmission takes place at the VIRTUAL semantic level, some central processing takes place and the data source would be PARTIAL.

2.4.3 Multiple Associations

In Sect. 2.3.1 it was noted that effort was to be concentrated on studying and classifying the associations in an application according to the graphical information being transferred and the networking services required to transfer that graphical information. This was motivated by the fact that applications might contain more than one association and that these associations might be characterized differently. This section describes a number of applications (information about which was collected during the extension of the work) that contain multiple associations and explores how these associations and their relationships can be characterized using the taxonomy framework.

Numerical Solution of Turbulent Flows. An application from the Aerospatial Department at the Politechnico di Milano illustrates the use of two associations in the numerical solution of turbulent flows. The description of the application actually relates to its future development when it is planned to convert the application from one being entirely non-graphical and running on a supercomputer to a distributed graphical application utilizing both a supercomputer and workstations.

The experimentor working through a visualization process on the workstation initiates the simulation on the supercomputer and provides input (either graphics or graphics related application data). A simulation process, in turn, requests the geometry model from the geometry database held on another workstation. The results of the simulation are returned to the workstation used by the experimentor for examination by the visualization process (capable of significant processing). This architecture is portrayed in Fig. 2.3 (note the direction of the arrow indicates the direction of the control).

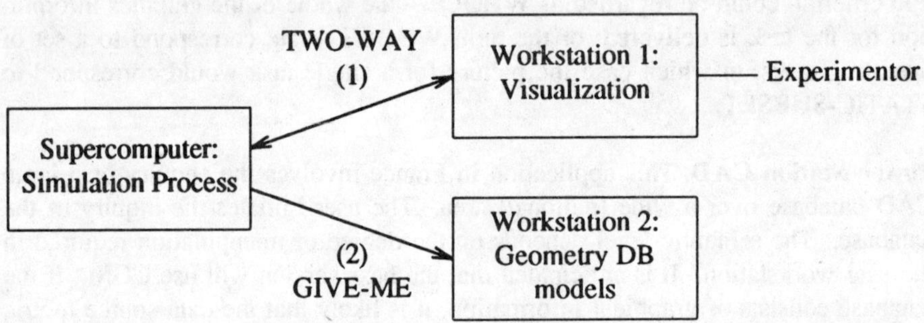

Fig. 2.3. Architecture for Turbulent Flow Application

The two associations are performing separate functions and need to be characterized separately. The values of the metrics for each of the functions are as follows:

Association 1

Semantic content:	a value between VIRTUAL and GRAPHICS RELATED[1]
Dimensions:	HIGHER (3 Euclidean dimensions plus data space dimensions)
Data source:	COMPLETE
Control:	TWO-WAY[2]
Selection criterion:	WHOLE
Quality of Service:	
data volume:	$(10^7, 10^6)$
transaction time:	MINUTES
transaction interval:	HOURS
acceptable error rate:	SPECIFIED-ACCEPTABLE

Note 1: The design is not yet complete and so a more precise value is not possible. This is discussed in Sect. 2.4.5.

Note 2: Association 1 is indicated as TWO-WAY. This is acceptable as long as the graphics input and output are at the same semantic level. If the semantic levels are different, two associations need to be created.

Association 2

Semantic content:	GRAPHICS-RELATED
Dimensions:	3D (Euclidean)
Data source:	COMPLETE
Control:	GIVE-ME
Selection criterion:	WHOLE[1]
Quality of service:	
data volume	$(10^5, 10^4)$
transaction time:	SECONDS to MINUTES
transaction interval:	HOURS
acceptable error rate:	SPECIFIED-ACCEPTABLE

Note 1: Depending upon how the geometry database is organized, it is quite likely that the selection criterion would actually be STATIC-SUBSET or even DYNAMIC-SUBSET.

Document Retrieval. Another application illustrating the use of two separate associations comes from an ESPRIT I project and relates to document retrieval. The information concerning the application was obtained from a German company.

The application is concerned with retrieving technical documents which may contain simple graphics and includes indexing and abstracting these documents. The retrieval software searches documents on a number of machines (currently local) and displays the documents on X Windows displays. The graphics included in the documents are mainly schematics (with a few boxes, circles, text and connecting lines) and may be scaled by the user but not modified. The user selects documents by means of keywords and it is documents that are transferred (with the graphics embedded). The architecture of the application is shown in Fig. 2.4. Associations labelled 1 all have the same characteristics and the precise number of them is immaterial. Association 2 is quite different. The values of the metrics for each type of association are as follows.

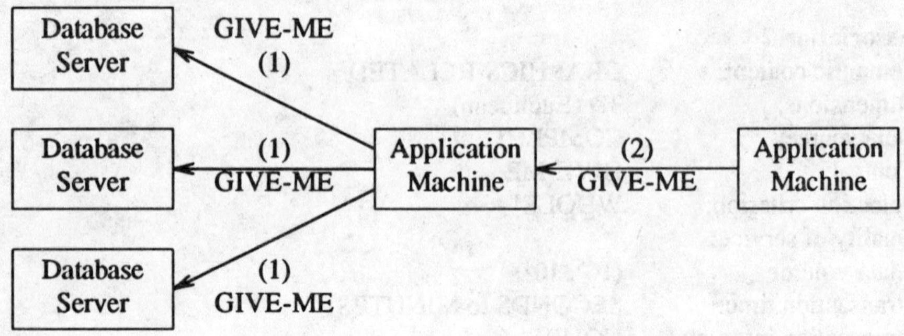

Fig. 2.4. Architecture for Document Retrieval Application

Association 1

Semantic content:	GRAPHICS-RELATED (Whole documents are transferred which may contain embedded graphics)
Dimensionality:	2D (Relates to the graphics contained in the document)
Data source:	COMPLETE
Control:	GIVE-ME
Selection criterion:	STATIC-SUBSET or DYNAMIC-SUBSET[1]
Quality of service:	
data volume:	Imprecise
transaction time:	SECONDS to MINUTES
transaction interval:	SECONDS to MINUTES
acceptable error rate:	SPECIFIED-ACCEPTABLE

Possible standards: FTAM with a document type for 'documents' (incorporating CGM graphics) would be appropriate.

Note 1: If the selection is based on defined keywords known to the database, the value is STATIC-SUBSET. If, however, locating the keywords involves searching the documents, the value would be DYNAMIC-SUBSET. This shows how this metric can be addressed to more than graphics data.

Association 2

Semantic content:	REALIZATION?
Dimensionality:	2D
Data source:	COMPLETE?
Control:	GIVE-ME?
Selection criterion:	WHOLE
Quality of Service:	
data volume:	Imprecise
transaction time:	
transaction interval:	
acceptable error rate:	SPECIFIED-ACCEPTABLE

Possible standards: Current service provided by X Windows: might CGI over Terminal Management or some such be the Open System Standard of the future?

Remote Sensing. NERC in the UK have a remote sensing application where the subject of interest is the sea temperature and the amount of plankton. The satellite data are transmitted to the receiving station in Dundee where geometric corrections are applied and the corrected data sent to Plymouth. The data take the form of 512×512 8-bit images in 3 bands. At Plymouth the images are overlaid with coast-line data currently in vector form. The composite images may then be queried by a ship in the region covered by the image. This leads to the architecture depicted in Fig. 2.5.

The data are at different semantic levels in the different associations. In the first association, the semantic level is graphics-related application data (the coordinate system may not even be well-defined as it will probably contain the results of optical distortions) and the control is TAKE-THIS. In the second association the semantic level will be lower, the coordinate system will be well-defined as a result of the geometric correction and will be a coordinate system to which the coast-line data can be related. Note that despite being an image, the semantic level will not be REALIZATION as the image is at a level where the coast-line data in vector form can be overlaid. This implies a semantic level of CONSTRUCTION or VIRTUAL. It is likely that the semantic level of the data requested by the ship is at a lower level again as it is requesting the composite image for display. The data will not need to be further processed. However, one could imagine a scenario where the ship requested a dynamic subset of the composite image (the area around the ship) which would best be done at the VIRTUAL level. Different image transfer standards (or different facets of the same standard) would be required for the different associations.

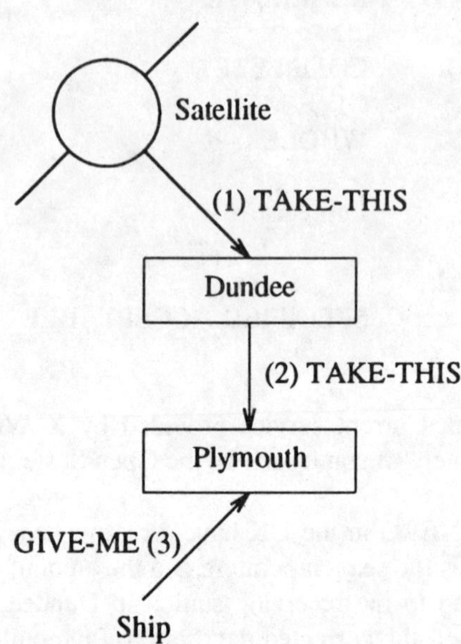

Fig. 2.5. Architecture for Remote Sensing Application

Remote Computation I. Multiple associations can be seen in a different light in an application from the University of Nice. The application makes use of remote computation and the necessity for multiple associations is on account of the differing semantic levels in the two directions of what, at first sight, might seem to be a single association. The application is in the area of education and research. From the application viewpoint the architecture is as shown in Fig. 2.6. (In practice, other workstations are involved in interfacing the local area network (LAN) to the Metropolitan Area Network (MAN) and in interfacing the MAN to the mainframe but these are only of concern to the lower layers of the network services.)

The workstation transmits GRAPHICS-RELATED data to the mainframe, across association 1 using TAKE-THIS control, for processing. When the processing is complete, the process on the mainframe transmits CGM files (VIRTUAL semantic level data) back to the workstation, again using TAKE-THIS control. If the data being transferred in the two directions were at the same semantic level, this application could have been classified as an application with a simple TWO-WAY association. Once the original data has been sent to the mainframe, the control could be interpreted as GIVE-ME by the workstation as a process is being instigated and the results are required to be returned. This was an area of discussion and indicates more study is needed in this area.

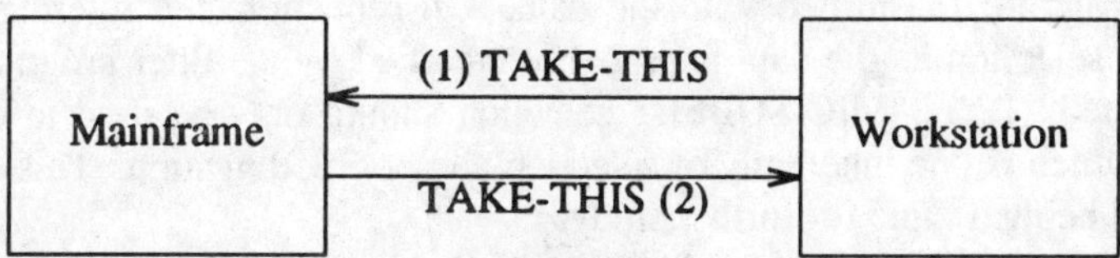

Fig. 2.6. Architecture for Remote Computation Application

Analysis of Spectrometric Data. A similar style of working to that discussed in the previous section, though less sophisticated, was perceived in an application concerned with the analysis of spectrometric data. The data from the spectrometer are collected on a PC and stored on a workstation. Complex filter operations are defined on the workstation and transmitted with the data for execution on a compute-server. The results are transmitted back to the workstation for display.

A graphic representation of the raw data is viewed on the workstation. The operator thinks of an appropriate filter and modifies the filter program to perform this particular filter operation. The data and program are transferred to the compute-server for execution and the results returned to the workstation. The results are displayed. The operator either thinks of a new filter or returns to view the raw data again and the process starts again at the appropriate stage. This is continued until the operator is satisfied with the result. The whole operation can be depicted as in Fig. 2.7.

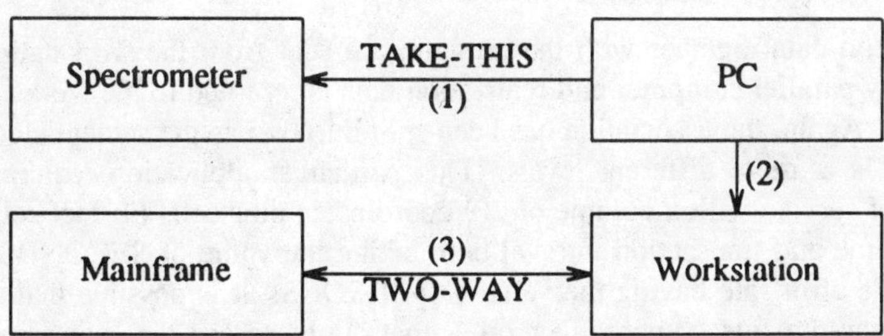

Fig. 2.7. Architecture for Spectrometric Analysis Application

Association 3 has been represented as a TWO-WAY association as the data being carried in each direction is at the same semantic level, namely GRAPHICS-RELATED. This applies both to the raw data and to the filtered data. If more control was required over where the filtered data was to be sent (for example, stored on the compute server) then two TAKE-THIS associations could have been used as in the previous application.

An alternative view of the association is that it uses GIVE-ME control with a selection criterion of DYNAMIC-SUBSET, where the dynamic subset is specified by the program transmitted with the data. On reflection, the filtering does not represent selection as the data is probably modified by the filter program and not just selected. DYNAMIC-SUBSET selection should only be used to describe a process which is one inherently of selection and not modification. This does point to control being a topic for further study.

Another interesting point raised by this application is that it uses an ethernet and the acceptable error rate was specified as DONT-BOTHER but with additional comment 'There are errors appearing due to overload on the networks and something should be done about it although we can live with the error rate.' This seems to match exactly the idea of SPECIFIED-ACCEPTABLE where the limit specified is just about to be reached!

Remote Computation II. A further example of remote computation was reported from the Institut Non Lineaire de Nice and relates to research in mathematics. The architecture for this example is shown in Fig. 2.8.

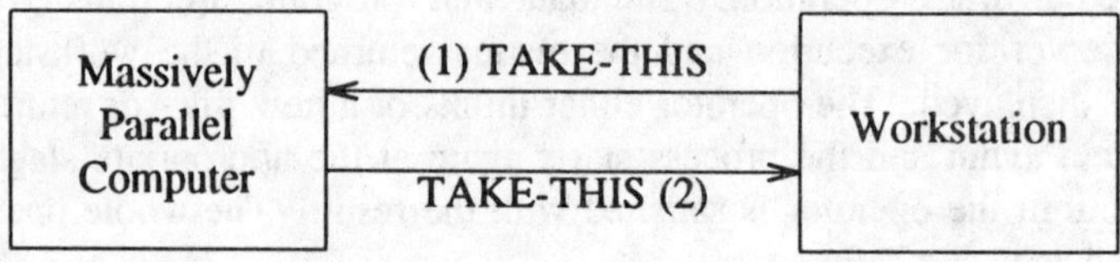

Fig. 2.8. Architecture for Remote Computation Application

Application data together with the program are sent from the workstation to the massively parallel computer and realization data is returned to the workstation for viewing. Again, the association has been split into two as the semantic content of the data is at quite different levels. This particular application requires a high quality of service with a volume of 10^5 coordinates plus cells (in fact cells), transaction time and transaction interval both taking the value of SECONDS and the acceptable error rate having the value NO-ERRORS. It is possible that there are timing requirements (synchronization?) that apply across the two associations. Further study in this area could prove fruitful.

2.4.4 Semantic Content of Image Data

A number of reasons make images a subject worth further study:

(1) This area has received less attention in the Computer Graphics Reference Model than other graphics primitives.
(2) Image data is often perceived as being at the REALIZATION semantic level, as it can be displayed directly, but, depending on accompanying data, it can exist at a number of semantic levels each with different possible manipulations.
(3) Many de facto standard image formats are in use as a means of exchange, as well as a number of formal but specialized standard image formats, such as those devised for the printing industry.
(4) The large volumes of observational data available in this form.

Two applications will be studied here. A further application was described in Sect. 2.4.3.

REALIZATION – Quality Colour Publishing. REALIZATION semantic content permits no manipulations by the receiver. Although this may seem to be a disadvantage, certain applications operate with identical equipment specifications and require precise facsimiles, centrally controlled. The data are already in a form that the receiver requires.

Quality colour publishing is an example of this. In this application, a complete issue of a colour magazine is prepared at one site in the USA and distributed nationally via satellite to several other sites for printing (see Fig. 2.9). Continuous tone colour is achieved by using a system of 12×12 microdots.

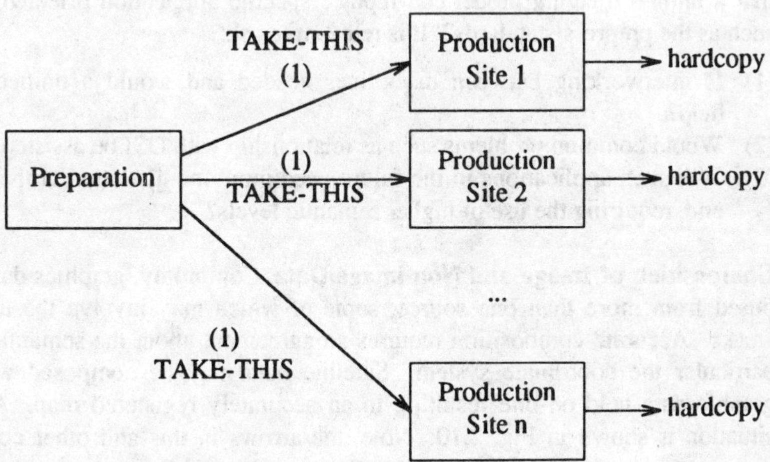

Fig. 2.9. Architecture for Quality Publishing Application

Each association carries the same information.

Association 1

Semantic content:	REALIZATION
Dimensions:	2D (2 Euclidean)
Data source:	COMPLETE
Control:	TAKE-THIS
Selection criterion:	WHOLE
Quality of service:	
data volume:	$(10^6, 10^0)$[1]
transaction time[2]	
transaction interval[2]	

Note 1: these figures are per page; 150 dots/inch on an A4 page; there are 64 pages.

Note 2: The main factor is the desire to respond to news stories as close to their occurrence as possible. Wish to transfer an image in MINUTES. Acceptable error rate: a small number of undetected errors is acceptable.

Possible standards: The current position is that the images are presented in the form of a colour prepress standard produced by the ANSC IT8 committee. For networking this is over X.25. With this demanding application, data compression is important and a lossless predictive compression technique is used which can reduce the transmission requirements by up to 10 times.

Imaging proposals are being made within ISO/IEC JTC1/SC24. Is it intended that a unified imaging model can replace specific application oriented standards such as the prepress standards? It is relevant to ask:

(1) Is interworking between disciplines needed and would a unified standard help?
(2) Would common problems such as relationship with OSI be assisted?
(3) Will such applications in the future need more manipulation at the receiving end, requiring the use of higher semantic levels?

Composition of Image and Non-image Data. Commonly, graphics data is composed from more than one source, some of which may involve the use of networks. Accurate composition requires an agreement about the semantic level, in particular the coordinate system. Satellite data may be composed with cartographic data held on-line resulting in an accurately registered map. A possible situation is shown in Fig. 2.10. Note, the arrows in this and other composition diagrams, indicate flow of data, rather than control as before.

If both sets of data originate from network associations, it is not necessary for the coordinate systems across the two associations to agree; it is only necessary for the coordinate systems on both associations to be acceptable to the composition process.

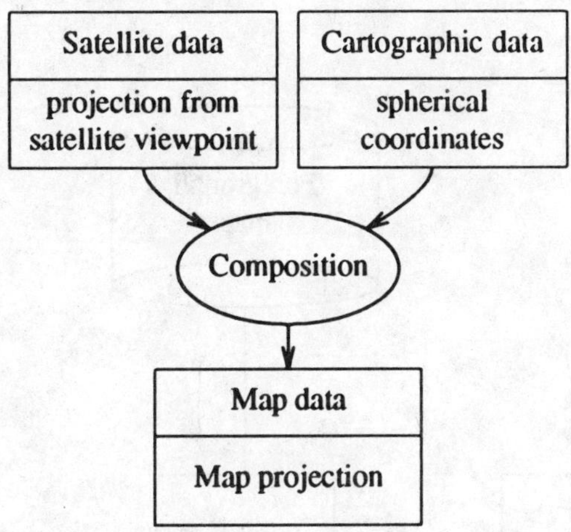

Fig. 2.10. Architecture for 'Composition' Application

An example is a C^{3}I application. In this application, a workstation composes together a background map which varies infrequently and a foreground map which changes in response to messages from the field. The components and associations are shown in Fig. 2.11.

Association 1 – transfer of background map

Semantic content:	LOGICAL[1]
Dimensions:	2D
Data source:	COMPLETE[2]
Control:	GIVE-ME
Selection criterion:	STATIC-SUBSET[3]
Quality of service:	
data volume:	$(10^6, 10^0)$
transaction time:	SECONDS
transaction interval:	MINUTES
acceptable error rate:	NONE

Note 1: Semantic content: the difference between REALIZATION and LOGICAL in this application is that REALIZATION would describe a bit-map version of the background map tailored to a specific device of known capabilities whereas LOGICAL would describe a bit-map which could be sent to a device-independent window system with some matters unresolved – such as the colour table.

Note 2: The data source is COMPLETE on the basis that the background map already completely exists and does not change in the course of the association.

Note 3: The selection criterion metric could be DYNAMIC-SUBSET if arbitrary regions of the background map were selected.

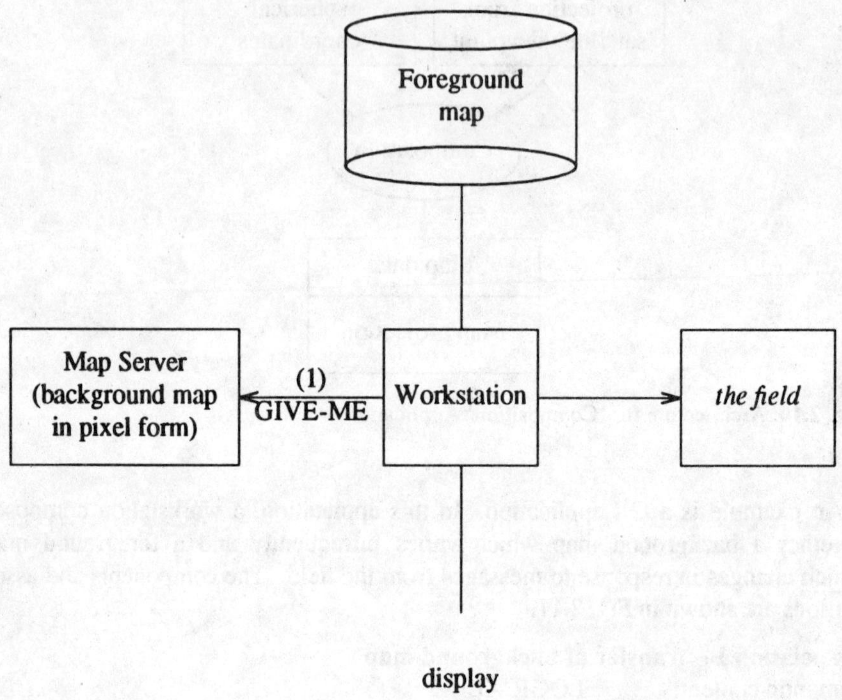

Fig. 2.11. Architecture for C^3 Application

Composition: The workstation displays the map, resulting from the composition in the workstation as shown in Fig. 2.12. The association between the workstation and the 'field' conveys messages the nature of which will not be discussed here. These are conveyed over X.25 WAN and radio links.

2.4.5 Design and Analysis Aid

With an existing application, the classification provides a technique for describing the architecture of the distributed graphics. For an application being designed, the classification not only does that, but provides a tool for describing and comparing the design alternatives.

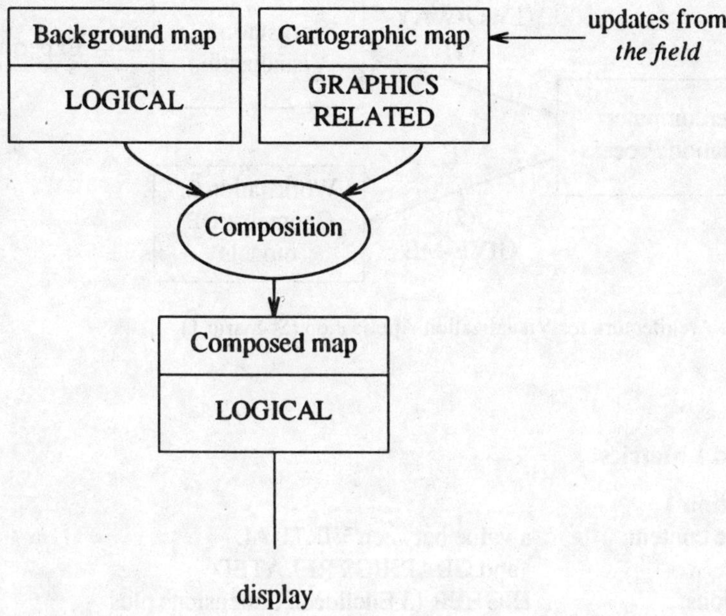

Fig. 2.12. Architecture for C^3 Application (Association 1)

The application from the Aerospatial Department at the Politechnico di Milano described in Sect. 2.4.3 illustrates this. Just one scenario was described there.

Two scenarios were reported in the original interview and an additional scenario (although not plausible) is presented for illustrative purposes. The architecture of each scenario is illustrated below. The essential difference between the scenarios is where the geometry database function is placed. In scenario 1 (see Fig. 2.13) it is in a second workstation; in scenario 2 (see Fig. 2.14), it is in the supercomputer; and in scenario 3 (see Fig. 2.15), the visualization and geometry database functions are in the same workstation. It will be seen that, although the physical configurations are different, the metric values remain the same in each scenario.

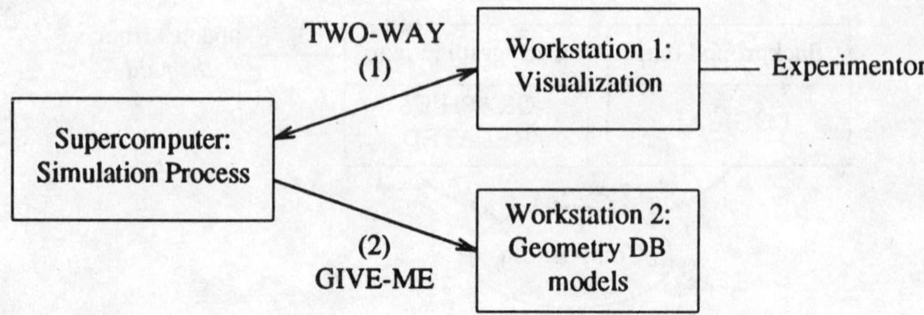

Fig. 2.13. Architecture for Visualization Application (Scenario 1)

Scenario 1 Metrics

Association 1

Semantic content:	a value between VIRTUAL and GRAPHICS RELATED[1]
Dimensions:	HIGHER (3 Euclidean dimensions plus data space dimensions)
Data source:	COMPLETE
Control:	TWO-WAY[2]
Selection criterion:	WHOLE
Quality of service:	
data volume:	$(10^7, 10^6)$
transaction time:	MINUTES
transaction interval:	HOURS
acceptable error rate:	SPECIFIED-ACCEPTABLE

Note 1: The design is not yet complete and a number of different values of the semantic content metric are possible (see Table 2.3). The choice of semantic content depends on network bandwidth, how much local manipulation is required without recourse to the network, the power of the workstation and the supercomputer, etc. Lower semantic levels than those listed might be used if only a viewing process was running on the workstation.

Table 2.3. Possible Semantic Levels

Data transferred	Corresponding semantic level	Workstation action
geometry of the model and solution data	GRAPHICS-RELATED	selects a visualization technique and displays it: the techniques and associated parameters can be altered by the workstation
constituent parts of the model	CONSTRUCTION	constructs a scene of the model parts; their relative positions and orientations may be altered by the workstation
graphical data resulting from visualization techniques	VIRTUAL	renders the graphical data: viewing parameters may be altered by the workstation

Note 2: Association 1 is indicated as TWO-WAY. This is acceptable as long as the graphics input and output are at the same semantic level. If the semantic levels are different, two associations need to be created.

Association 2

Semantic content: GRAPHICS-RELATED
Dimensions: 3D
Data source: COMPLETE
Control: GIVE-ME
Selection criterion: WHOLE[1]
Quality of Service:
data volume: $(10^5, 10^4)$
transaction time: SECONDS to MINUTES
transaction interval: HOURS
acceptable error rate: SPECIFIED ACCEPTABLE

Note 1: Depending upon how the geometry database is organized, it is quite likely that the selection criterion would actually be STATIC-SUBSET or even DYNAMIC-SUBSET.

Scenario 2

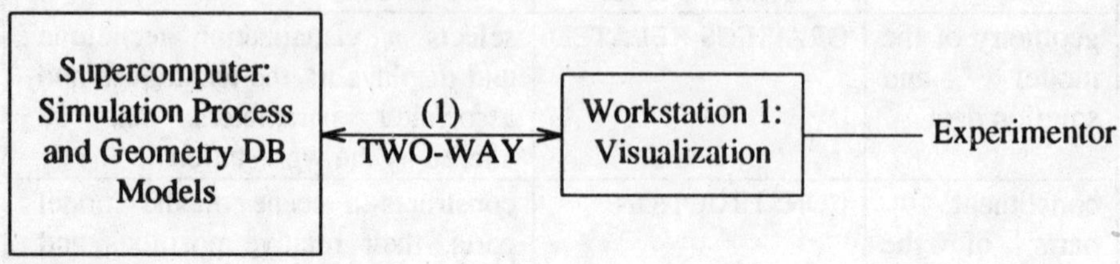

Fig. 2.14. Architecture for Visualization Application (Scenario 2)

Scenario 2 Metrics

There is just one association and that is the same as scenario 1 association 1.

Scenario 3

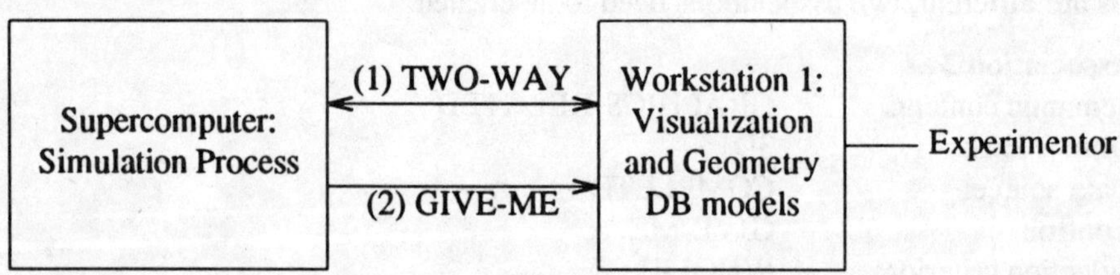

Fig. 2.15. Architecture for Visualization Application (Scenario 3)

Scenario 3 Metrics

Here there are two links as in scenario 1, but both are between the supercomputer and the workstation. The values of the metrics are the same as in scenario 1. Fig. 2.15 makes it clear that this scenario places a more severe load on the network connection and on the workstation's resources. However, this configuration may be more suitable for development.

2.5 Conclusions

2.5.1 Summary

In order to achieve the integration of graphics and OSI standards and to meet the requirements of applications, it is necessary to understand the needs of applications to transfer graphical information and the networking services required to support this. A major component of the ARGOSI project has been to derive a taxonomy framework for applications based on a set of metrics describing their use of graphics and networking.

This understanding has led to an improvement in the understanding of application needs in a number of areas.

(1) The taxonomy was initially derived from surveys made earlier in the task. Subsequent application interviews have been made with the knowledge of this initial taxonomy and it has been clarified in a number of areas. It has also been found that it provides a methodology for analysing application requirements for distributed graphics.

(2) Work in the final phase of the task has confirmed the importance of understanding a distributed application, by creating multiple associations where necessary.

(3) The use of the taxonomy as a design aid, to analyse several scenarios has been illustrated in this chapter.

(4) In relation to standards, the importance of subsets of information was revealed in a significant number of applications. The appearance of this early on in the task gave added weight to the Project's work on CGM over FTAM and subsequent work has confirmed the importance of subsets selected before transmission. This question is in principle not restricted to CGM. Subsets are relevant to the proposed imaging standard and to graphics-related application encoding layers.

(5) With regard to the metric 'semantic content of data transferred across the network', both extremes (APPLICATION-DATA and REALIZATION) have occurred in the applications described in the interviews and are reported here. The two top layers (APPLICATION-DATA, GRAPHICS-RELATED) have encompassed a variety of requirements, depending on the application. Therefore it is not possible to be specific about particular standards for these layers, without an understanding of the application concerned.

The taxonomy framework has been described together with its derivation. It is believed to be a major step forward in the field though there remain a few unanswered questions. This is discussed further in the next section.

2.5.2 Future Development

After a certain amount of elaboration of the taxonomy framework, confidence is being gained in the set of metrics that has been derived. In some cases, however, the set of values for a metric may need further refinement. For example, it may be necessary to distinguish between three Cartesian coordinates plus time and four dimensional homogeneous coordinates within the value 4D of the dimensionality metric. The values of the metrics should be studied further.

The quality of service metric needs further study; for example, how does it relate to the taxonomy framework. Consideration needs to be given as to whether image fidelity should be included as a component and whether this covers the requirements for image compression. There is also an issue of whether geographical area is an important aspect of quality of service.

The control metric also needs further study. It is important to understand that 'control' here is used in the sense of the style of control required by applications. A particular style of control at this level might be realized by networking services which exhibit other styles of control at lower levels in the network architecture. There is scope for a deeper understanding and characterization of association control.

The motivation for constructing the taxonomy framework was to classify the requirements of applications so that they could be studied to see if they were met by the current set of Graphics and OSI Standards. However, while the work was being carried out, it was discovered that many applications could be implemented in a number of different ways which used different graphics and networking services.

Sect. 2.4.5 has shown how the taxonomy framework can be used as a design aid, by exploring how different architectures map onto the framework. The framework and its mapping onto required services can then be used to examine the trade-offs between different architectural solutions. There is scope for further work here in exploring the effectiveness of this approach, and for putting the trade-off analysis on a more quantitative footing.

The work has also brought to light a number of areas which no combination of existing standards addresses, or are only partially addressed. An example of the latter is the support of interactive working using the CGI standard, for which no harmonized networking services support currently exists. An example of the former is a graphics standard for the transfer of a dynamic subset of data. There is a link to work in spatial data management which is worthy of further exploration.

The postal questionnaire gave evidence of much interest in X-windows. There was insufficient detail to determine whether this implies a significant requirement for windowing over a network as X windows can also be used locally.

2.5.3 Acknowledgements

We acknowledge the help of those who returned questionnaires in the postal survey. We further appreciate those who took time and patience to be interviewed by one of the partners in the work.

References

1. France Telecom (July 1990), *Reseau Recherche Haut Debit Ile de France - Analyse des Besoins,* France Telecom.

3 Network Connectivity Study

3.1 Introduction

Since the ARGOSI application prototype was to use Public Data Networks, it was necessary to assess whether this was likely to be feasible. Methods of testing reliability and performance of the connections between partners on Public Data Networks (PSPDNs) were developed. Although the experiment was largely completed before the application prototype was begun, the method of testing and the method of presenting results are of continuing interest. The report of the activity is included here unchanged (including the use of the future tense) and reflects the state of PSPDNs in September 1990.

There were two reasons for choosing to use PSPDNs for the prototype application:

- It is wished to demonstrate the prototype application in as general a context as possible. This means that it should be possible to demonstrate it across international boundaries (to demonstrate the 'European' nature of the work) and between as many partner sites as possible (to demonstrate the 'Open Systems' nature of the work). These aims dictate the use of publicly available facilities – it is infeasible to use private, leased lines (for example) within the resources of the project.
- It is wished to demonstrate that publicly available facilities *can* be used to offer useful services in conjunction with ISO Graphics and Networking Standards. There seems little point in producing a demonstration that uses *only* specialized network services, as this would be a partial non-fulfillment of this aim. Additionally, one result of the demonstration work should be to identify the weaknesses of the currently available facilities, and to make recommendations as to how these can be overcome. To do this 'real' service conditions must be experienced.

It is, of course, recognized that there are potentially serious problems to be faced regarding the bandwidth and reliability offered by the European PSPDNs, particularly when international connectivity is sought. Therefore this activity was designed with the aim of quantifying these aspects in the light of three sources of information:

- the initial requirements for data transfer provided by work done on the prototype application;
- existing available data on the performance and reliability of international PSPDN working;
- a programme of specific testing between the sites of Partners expecting to participate in the demonstration of the application prototype.

3.2 Networking Requirements of the Application Prototype

As a result of work done on the classification of applications, the project decided that the application prototype should take the form of a Geographical Information System. The aim will be to model a system whereby land-based freight operators may obtain information on likely transport difficulties due to adverse weather, roadworks etc in any European country. This information will be distributed via wide-area networks, with the assumption that it is effectively publicly available.

The basic model will be one whereby static information (road maps etc) will be stored at the display point. There will be a database of 'difficulties' associated with a particular country, held in that country. The user software will interrogate the database to obtain the relevant information, and overlay this graphically on the appropriate map. Thus a relatively small amount of information will need to be transferred in a transaction.

It is intended that the data will be transferred as a Computer Graphics Metafile (CGM), or more precisely, that it will be abstracted from a CGM held in the 'difficulties' database. To do this, the CGM structure will need to be mapped onto a FTAM representation, and FTAM will be used for the data transfer.

The structure of each database is intended to be a series of 2 degree (geographical) squares; each square will be in a separately accessible picture of a CGM. Initial estimates have been made for a 'typical' complexity of a query on the database as follows:

- one query involves ~6 squares;
- each square contains ~30 pieces of information concerning 'difficulties';
- each piece of information can be coded into ~120 octets.

This leads to an estimate of a FTAM transfer of ~21 Kbytes to process a query. The initial requirement was that this transfer can be achieved in 5 seconds (best case) to 15 seconds (worst case).

In terms of underlying network bandwidth, this implies that the FTAM process will need to be able to deliver 34.5 Kbit/s (best case) to 11.5 Kbit/s (worst case).

It should be noted that this estimate assumes that it is necessary to transfer the *whole* CGM before display of the information contained therein can begin to take place. It may be possible that the display can be built up as the CGM arrives at the receiving computer; this might ease the response time requirement as far as the user is concerned. Whether this is possible will depend on whether the receiving FTAM software will allow access to data as it arrives, and on whether the CGM can be interpreted 'on the fly' in this manner. Further studies are being made in this area.

3.3 PSPDN Connections and Host Equipment at Partner Sites

The first task undertaken was for each Partner to investigate the X.25 facilities that could reasonably be available at his site, as well as the possible availability of application-level software with which testing could be carried out. The results of these investigations were collated at the meeting of the Workpackage at GMD-FOKUS (Berlin) on 18 July 1989. The following is a summary.

COSI

COSI has a VAX 11/750 running VMS attached to ITAPAC (the Italian PSPDN). The VAX runs PSI Version 4.2 to provide X.25. The connection bandwidth is 9.6 Kbit/s; 19.2 Kbit/s could become available later.

GMD-FOKUS

GMD-FOKUS have a VAX 8530 running VMS and a Sun/3 running SunOS, both connected to DATEX-P (the West German PSPDN), using DEC's PSI software and Sun's Sunlink X.25 software respectively. The connection bandwidth is 9.6 Kbit/s, with 64 Kbit/s expected in the near future.

Hitec

Hitec is using a Sun 3/60 running SunOS attached to HELLASPAC (the Greek PSPDN). They are currently using a dial-up connection with a bandwidth of 1.2 Kbit/s. A permanent connection to the network has been ordered, but has yet to be installed. The connection bandwidth ordered is 4.8 Kbit/s, although it is expected that this could be upgraded to 9.6 Kbit/s. (By the end of the project a permanent 9.6Kbit/s X.25 connection had been installed.)

INRIA

INRIA has a Pyramid running OSX, connected to TRANSPAC (the French PSPDN). However, this connection is via INRIA's internal high-speed X.25 network. The effective connection bandwidth between the Pyramid and TRANSPAC depends on the route taken through the internal network; two links are available from the Pyramid, operating at 9.6 Kbit/s and 19.2 Kbit/s.

RAL

RAL expects to use a Sun/4 running SunOS. This is currently attached to JANET (the UK Joint Academic Network – a network used by academic researchers). The Sun has Sunlink X.25(1980) software, due to be upgraded to X.25(1984) during 1990. The current connection bandwidth is 9.6Kbit/s, although this could be upgraded to 64 Kbit/s if required. JANET is connected to PSS (the UK PSPDN) via a gateway, which is slow and not transparent in use (in particular it does not support the OSI Network Service, and is only transparent to a Network Service developed in the UK academic community). The current link between JANET and PSS operates at 9.6 Kbit/s. Therefore it might be more appropriate to install a direct connection to PSS from the Sun; this would be at 9.6 Kbit/s. It was decided not to order such a link immediately, pending the outcome of the feasibility study being undertaken. For the testing work reported here, a Pyramid running OSX was used. This was connected to JANET at 19.2 Kbit/s.

Tecsiel

Tecsiel has a HP 835 running HP UX connected to ITAPAC. The connection bandwidth is 9.6 Kbit/s; an upgrade to 19.2 Kbit/s is possible. There is also a VAX 11/780 connected at 2.4 Kbit/s. It is planned to run any OSI services on the HP 385, but to run any graphics services on a Sun/3 or Sun/4 attached to the same LAN as the HP (and currently connected via TCP/IP).

Thomson CSF

Thomson will use a UNIGRAPH running Unix System V. At the time the testing was carried out this was attached to TRANSPAC via an X.29 PAD; the PAD itself is connected to TRANSPAC at 19.2 Kbit/s, but the connection between the PAD and UNIGRAPH is at 9.6 Kbit/s. The PAD was removed and the UNIGRAPH connected directly to TRANSPAC at 19.2 Kbit/s early in 1990.

In summary, therefore, the potential bandwidths available are as given in Table 3.1.

3.4 Performance and Reliability of PSPDNs

There is a shortage of reliable data on the genuine end-to-end performance delivered by PSPDNs. Figures available from the service providers normally relate to the performance of the network itself, and often are not available for international connections. Figures produced by network service users are often anecdotal, often obtained under non-reproducible conditions, and sometimes obtained merely to use in debate with a PTT rather than produced for disinterested reasons.

Table 3.1. Potential Bandwidths available at Partners' Sites

	4.8 Kbit/s	*9.6 Kbit/s*	*19.2 Kbit/s*	*48 Kbit/s*	*64 Kbit/s*
COSI		●	o		
GMD FOKUS		●			o
Hitec	●	o			
INRIA		●	●		
RAL		●			o
Tecsiel		●	o		
Thomson CSF		●	o		

('●' = currently available; 'o' = possibly/probably available in future.)

3.4.1 COSINE Performance Study

The COSINE Specification Phase recognized this situation, and commissioned an independent study (COSINE Study 6.2.2) in 1988. This study looked at file transfer performance over international PSPDN connections, involving sites in the United Kingdom, West Germany, Belgium and The Netherlands. These countries were chosen as having the highest bandwidth direct connections with each other. (France is also well served; information was not given for Italy or Greece.) Table 3.2 shows the connection bandwidths provided (figures in Kbit/s).

Table 3.2. International PSPDN Connection Bandwidths (COSINE Study 6.2.2)

	W Germany	*UK*	*France*	*Belgium*	*Netherlands*
W Germany	–	1×64 3×19.2	2×64	1×64 1× 9.6	1×64 2× 9.6
UK	1×64 3×19.2	–	2×19.2	1×64 2× 9.6	2× 9.6
France	2×64	2×19.2	–	2×48	2× 9.6
Belgium	1×64 1× 9.6	1×64 2× 9.6	2×48	–	1×64 2× 9.6
Netherlands	1×64 2× 9.6	2× 9.6	2× 9.6	1×64 2× 9.6	–

Extensive file transfer tests were conducted between these 4 countries, using 'Blue Book' file transfer. The following throughputs observed (from a sample of 327 transfers) are given in Table 3.3. The connection to the PSPDN at each site was 9.6 Kbit/s.

Table 3.3. Throughputs Between International PSPDNs (COSINE Study 6.2.2)

	Throughput (Kbit/s)	*% of Nominal Bandwidth*
Day	4.1 ± 1.4	42
Night	5.1 ± 1.8	53
All	4.6 ± 1.6	48

It was found during the test that the file transfer software at the participating UK site gave problems. Therefore figures excluding the UK were also given; Table 3.4 gives these.

Table 3.4. Throughputs Excluding the UK (COSINE Study 6.2.2)

	Throughput (Kbit/s)	*% of Nominal Bandwidth*
Day	5.3 ± 1.0	55
Night	6.8 ± 0.6	71
All	6.0 ± 1.2	63

From the survey of ARGOSI partners' own PSPDN connections shown earlier, it seems likely that bandwidths of 9.6 Kbit/s will normally be used, with no partner anticipating a slower connection than this. (This assumes that Hitec does upgrade to 9.6 Kbit/s.) Therefore it seems reasonable to anticipate an *effective* bandwidth between partners of approximately one-half of this nominal bandwidth. Based on this figure, the anticipated transfer time for the 'typical' transaction in the application prototype would be ~36 seconds i.e. approximately twice the required worst-case time. (It also needs to be remembered that the COSINE study looked at only a subset of the PSPDNs that would be used by the application prototype if all partners are involved – data are not available in particular for Italy and Greece.)

It must also be recognized that the estimate takes no account of the *call setup time* that might be needed to establish an FTAM session. This could be an important contribution to the overall time of a session when such a small amount of data is being transferred. (The COSINE study was conducted using 500 Kbyte transfers, thus minimizing the effect of the call setup overhead.) It seems likely that part of the work of the demonstration will be to study the best ways of dealing with the overhead of session establishment inherent in current OSI services.

3.4.2 COSINE Reliability Study

The COSINE study also attempted to quantify the reliability of the PSPDNs used in the trial, in terms of broken connections, or connections that failed to set up in the first place.

It is necessary to distinguish between errors due to the PSPDNs being used, and those due to the end-point hosts and/or their software. For the 327 transfers attempted, there were a total of 77 failures (i.e. the transfer had to be retried), broken down as shown in Table 3.5.

Table 3.5. Reliability of International PSPDN Connections (COSINE Study 6.2.2)

Network Level		*Higher Levels*	
network congestion	3	transport service failure	20
remote procedure error	10	FTP error	2
invalid packet type	3		
rejected by remote host	2		
remote host down	2		
network RESET	35		

The COSINE study counts only 'network congestion' errors as evidence of PSPDN failure, although 'remote procedure error' and 'invalid packet type' errors could conceivably be attributed to a malfunctioning PSPDN – it is not possible to determine this without detailed information. Even with these included, failures due to the PSPDN network service give a less than 5% failure rate.

A network RESET is not, strictly, a failure – the application should be able to recover from this and continue the session. However, 'Blue Book' file transfer implementations often abort the session in such an eventuality. Given the relatively high occurrence of these (11% in the sample), it seems that especial care must be taken to ensure that the application prototype implementation is resilient to events of this nature.

3.4.3 Availability of Higher Speed Services

There appear to be a number of initiatives to provide pilot implementations of higher speed services, some of which may be available for use by 'guinea pig' projects (e.g. the EBIT initiative to provide broadband ISDN for selected sites). However, the aim of the ARGOSI demonstration is to use services that are both widely and realistically available either now or in the near future.

With this in mind, the only candidate at the present time seems to be the International X.25 Interconnect (IXI) Project being developed as a Pilot by the COSINE Project. This aims to provide high quality (and high bandwidth) international links between national PSPDNs, and (where in existence) private research networks, of a number of European states. The Pilot will provide connections at 64 Kbit/s between countries, and should encompass all ARGOSI partner countries. The agreement between PTTs necessary to implement the Pilot has now been signed, and the intention is to start operating the Pilot during 1990.

The type of service envisaged for the application prototype would not fall within the operational remit of the IXI, which is concerned with services for the R&D community. However, it seems that the IXI is a good example of the type of publicly available service that can be expected in the next few years, and of course the research being carried out to build the application prototype does fall within the IXI remit.

It should be noted that the IXI will only concern itself with connections between countries, and that the Pilot will only provide 64 Kbit/s connections. (As shown earlier, there are already some 64 Kbit/s connections between PSPDNs provided by the PTTs.) This means that it cannot simply be assumed that much greater bandwidth will be available than currently attainable; in particular, the quality of the connection from a partner site to his PSPDN may act as a bottleneck. However, the IXI is likely to be relatively lightly loaded during the Pilot, and this may lead to the provision of better throughput than can be provided by the heavily loaded international PSPDN connections. The IXI should also provide a more reliable service than the PSPDNs, for the same reason.

The Project therefore decided that developments within the IXI were of potential interest, and should be monitored. However, it was decided that a definite decision as to its usefulness could not be made until such time as it had become a demonstrable reality in sufficient of the Partners' countries.

3.5 Development of a Testing Regime

It was decided that the quantities to be measured as a means of gauging suitability of the connection should be kept simple, viz:

- throughput obtained, both to user and total (at the network level);
- call setup times for sessions;
- success rate for initiated test sessions;
- detailed statistics for sessions that failed (reason for call clearance etc).

A number of test methodologies were looked at with these requirements in mind, based on which application-level software to use to conduct the tests. The advantages and disadvantages of each were summarized – these are given in Table 3.6.

(The option of using a fully-fledged OSI application such as FTAM or MHS was briefly considered at an earlier stage. It was rejected on the grounds that a disproportionate amount of effort would be needed to achieve interworking, before testing could begin.)

Table 3.6. Comparison of Testing Methodologies

	Advantages	*Disadvantages*
Above X.25	capable of precise network-level statistics	involves writing of software, non-portable between systems
Above TP0	involves writing software, but easier and more portable than writing at the network level	a TS interface is not available at all sites
Above X.29	available at all sites as part of X.25 software packages	not easy to use to obtain the statistics required
Above uucp	available on all Unix systems	of no intrinsic interest to ARGOSI; not all partners have a Unix system

It was decided that the limited amount of effort available dictated the use of the only software common and available to all sites – X.29. It was decided that testing would be done by listing a large file (~150 Kbyte) over a terminal session set up via X.29. This would provide reasonable throughput and call-failure statistics. It would not, however, yield call setup time statistics, due to the interactive nature of the sessions involved.

3.6 Results of Throughput and Reliability Tests

Tests based upon the X.29 regime described in the preceding Section were carried out during November and December 1989. The Partners taking part were COSI, GMD-FOKUS, INRIA, RAL, Tecsiel and Thomson. Hitec was unable to participate as the X.25 connection to its site was not in place. RAL's participation was more limited, as the testing could only be carried out with equipment and conditions that approximated to those expected for any demonstration of the application prototype. Thus it was not wished to expend an inordinate amount of effort on this.

The methodology used was for each Partner to log onto each of his colleagues' systems using X.29. He then listed the agreed text file onto the screen of his local terminal. The system clock at the remote site was used to provide a timing for the listing, and hence the effective bit rate end-to-end, via simple command scripts. Thus the direction of data flow used to measure bandwidth was *opposite* to that direction in which the call was made.

Besides throughput measurements, records were kept of each call that failed either during the transfer or (more usually) at the call set-up stage. The clearing code of each failure, where ascertainable, was used to categorize the failure.

Due to the limited amount of resource available (both in effort and in funds for network charges), it was decided that each Partner should attempt to perform 10 such listings from each other Partner's system. All calls were made during normal working hours, so as to simulate the sort of conditions expected for the demonstration of the application prototype.

To determine that the throughput figures seen were not simply a reflection of bottlenecks in host performance, loopback tests were also carried out at each system, through its local packet-switch exchange.

Naturally, some difficulties were encountered during the tests. Where specific to a particular site, these are elaborated below, where that site's results are discussed. However, there were two problems which could potentially have affected the results collected by all sites.

- Unexpectedly low throughput figures were obtained for data emanating from the VAX/VMS systems used by certain Partners (COSI, GMD-FOKUS, Tecsiel). Investigation showed that the problem was that by default at these sites the VMS system was transmitting X.29 data without ensuring that each packet was filled completely. This was unrealistic in the context of bulk-data transfer, so this default behaviour was altered. (It was a matter of disabling the parameter *NOHOLD* for the session, and instead setting the parameter *HOLD* to a value '1'.) This alteration led to results more in keeping with expectations, and these latter *only* have been included in this report.
- At INRIA it was not possible to specify or know which of the two routes into and out of the system used was in fact used for any particular test. In the event this did not seem to make a noticeable difference, except for the loopback tests, as the local variations were swamped by other factors.

3.6.1 Throughput Results

This Section details the throughput results on a site-by-site basis. Collated summaries of the throughputs into and out of each site can be found in Appendix 1.

Loopback Tests. Table 3.7 gives the figures obtained for loopback tests through the local packet-switch exchange at each site.

Table 3.7. Throughput Figures – Loopback Tests

	Bandwidth (Kbit/s)	*No. of tests*	*mean (bit/s)*	*worst (bit/s)*	*median (bit/s)*	*best (bit/s)*
COSI	9.6	10	*4523*	2182	4030	9211
GMD	9.6	10	*7101*	6970	7105	7164
INRIA	9.6/19.2	4	*7041*	4386	6647	10484
RAL	19.2	10	*8930*	8832	8955	8955
Tecsiel	9.6	11	*5819*	3674	5328	7369
Thomson	9.6	9	*7459*	7369	7454	7497

A particularly wide spread in results was obtained for INRIA. This is believed to be due to the existence of two different bandwidth links to the system used (see above).

Otherwise no evidence could be seen that host problems would affect unduly the results obtained.

Results for COSI. Table 3.8 gives the figures obtained for bulk data flowing into COSI.

Table 3.8. Throughput Figures – Data ***into*** COSI

	No. of tests	*No. failed*	*mean (bit/s)*	*worst (bit/s)*	*median (bit/s)*	*best (bit/s)*
GMD	10	0	*2125*	569	1791	3884
INRIA	12	4	*2168*	1088	1636	4120
RAL	10	0	*1804*	691	1468	2957
Tecsiel	10	0	*4214*	2178	4228	5441
Thomson	11	3	*2389*	656	2543	4004

The throughputs obtained were relatively poor, with the exception of the figure for data from Tecsiel. The system used by COSI was a VAX at Milan Polytechnic and was at times heavily loaded. However, the reasonably good figure obtained from Tecsiel suggests that this was not the cause of the generally low figures. It seems more likely that the international links out of ITAPAC are responsible.

Results for GMD-FOKUS. Table 3.9 gives the figures obtained for bulk data flowing into GMD-FOKUS.

Table 3.9. Throughput Figures – Data ***into*** GMD-FOKUS

	No. of tests	*No. failed*	*mean (bit/s)*	*worst (bit/s)*	*median (bit/s)*	*best (bit/s)*
COSI	12	1	*2899*	1745	2791	4200
INRIA	34	2	*5730*	4866	5783	6448
RAL	0	--	--	--	--	--
Tecsiel	11	0	*3355*	2069	3003	5158
Thomson	30	1	*7342*	6170	7454	7541

A result for data from RAL was not obtained due to parity problems experienced when attempting to log into the RAL system. This was thought to be due to an interaction at the JANET/PSS gateway.

Otherwise, the throughputs obtained were reasonable, with better performance from TRANSPAC than from ITAPAC.

Results for INRIA. Table 3.10 gives the figures obtained for bulk data flowing into INRIA.

Table 3.10. Throughput Figures – Data ***into*** INRIA

	No. of tests	*No. failed*	*mean (bit/s)*	*worst (bit/s)*	*median (bit/s)*	*best (bit/s)*
COSI	8	0	*1764*	858	1329	4173
GMD	9	0	*2982*	1788	3256	3533
RAL	8	0	*4904*	2930	5285	5681
Tecsiel	7	0	*2442*	1265	2063	3494
Thomson	7	0	*7402*	7046	7411	7541

The throughputs obtained to Thomson CSF were good; this was expected as the two sites are geographically close, and hence probably do not need a complex path through TRANSPAC to set up a call. Throughputs to DATEX-P and PSS were reasonable, to ITAPAC less good.

Results for RAL. Table 3.11 gives the figures obtained for bulk data flowing into RAL.

Table 3.11. Throughput Figures – Data ***into*** RAL

	No. of tests	*No. failed*	*mean (bit/s)*	*worst (bit/s)*	*median (bit/s)*	*best (bit/s)*
COSI	5	0	*3605*	3306	3685	3737
GMD	9	0	*3985*	2579	4386	4884
INRIA	16	6	*3681*	3264	3711	4133
Tecsiel	0	--	--	--	--	--
Thomson	11	0	*4288*	3804	4200	5200

A result for Tecsiel was not obtained, due to problems in being able to set up a call with the correct address. The precise reason for this was not determined in the time available for testing.

The throughputs obtained were all reasonable, with a surprisingly good figure obtained for data from COSI in the light of the other tests.

Results for Tecsiel. Table 3.12 gives the figures obtained for bulk data flowing into Tecsiel.

Table 3.12: Throughput Figures – Data ***into*** Tecsiel

	No. of tests	*No. failed*	*mean (bit/s)*	*worst (bit/s)*	*median (bit/s)*	*best (bit/s)*
COSI	10	0	*3655*	2258	3827	4200
GMD	13	3	*3705*	2767	3503	5395
INRIA	13	5	*2893*	1070	3288	4042
RAL	10	1	*3017*	1953	3055	3861
Thomson	12	2	*2772*	934	2996	4042

The throughputs obtained were quite consistent, albeit not high, for data from all sites including COSI, which is also on ITAPAC. This contrasts with the behaviour found at COSI.

Results for Thomson CSF. Table 3.13 gives the figures obtained for bulk-data flowing into Thomson CSF. The throughputs obtained were good to INRIA (also on TRANSPAC), and to DATEX-P and PSS. Less good throughputs were obtained to both sites on ITAPAC.

Table 3.13. Throughput Figures – Data *into* Thomson CSF

	No. of tests	*No. failed*	*mean (bit/s)*	*worst (bit/s)*	*median (bit/s)*	*best (bit/s)*
COSI	4	1	*2935*	1210	3513	4081
GMD	4	0	*5550*	4922	5351	6575
INRIA	10	1	*5687*	5328	5511	6787
RAL	7	4	*4275*	2779	4672	5373
Tecsiel	4	1	*2548*	1137	2060	4446

The relatively small numbers of tests with data from COSI, GMD-FOKUS and Tecsiel are due to the discarding of a number of earlier results. This was due to the packet-filling problem described above.

3.6.2 Reliability

For the 307 calls and subsequent transfers attempted there were a total of 35 failures.

Call-failure data is analysed in Table 3.14. For the analysis the clearing cause, where reported, was examined. A value of '00' was taken to mean that a host had cleared the call, other values that a network problem had led to call clearance. Specifically, the value '05' was taken to signify 'network congestion'. Network congestion seems to be the most frequent problem. This is noticeable particularly at INRIA for incoming calls, and at Tecsiel for outgoing calls. In both these cases there are also instances of 'other' network failures; these too are possibly indicative of network overload.

Appendix 2 shows between which sites the failures were found.

3.7 Conclusions

The following conclusions can be drawn from the tests.

A general estimate of 3 Kbit/s is reasonable for the throughput to be expected across the Partner sites. This is in agreement with COSINE's file-transfer study – the figures are slightly worse, possibly due to the inclusion of ITAPAC sites in the present study.

Table 3.14. Reasons for Call Clearance, Analysed by Calling & Called Site

Calling site	*No. of calls made*	*Number failed*	*Reason for Call Failure*			
			rem. host failure	*network congestion*	*network other*	*unknown reason*
COSI	53	7	--	--	--	7
GMD	87	4	1	3	--	--
INRIA	39	0	--	--	--	--
RAL	41	6	2	1	3	--
Tecsiel	58	11	2	7	2	--
Thomson	29	7	1	--	--	6

Called site	*No. of calls received*	*Number failed*	*Reason for Call Failure*			
			loc. host failure	*network congestion*	*network other*	*unknown reason*
COSI	39	2	2	--	--	--
GMD	45	3	2	1	--	--
INRIA	85	18	2	6	5	5
RAL	35	5	--	1	--	4
Tecsiel	32	1	--	--	--	1
Thomson	71	6	--	3	--	3

The best throughput figures were between TRANSPAC and DATEX-P. The figures to and from PSS were acceptable, and probably would be bettered if the JANET/PSS gateway were not to be used. There did seem to be evidence of problems with international connections to ITAPAC, with Tecsiel (Pisa) fairing better than COSI (Milan) overall.

Network Congestion was quite severe at INRIA (although some was seen at Thomson CSF as well). Subsequent investigation showed that there were problems in this respect on INRIA's internal X.25 network, and it has been decided to use a different system for any development of the application prototype in order to ease the problems.

Network congestion was also apparent at Tecsiel on outgoing calls. In the absence of other evidence, it seems likely that a problem was being experienced within ITAPAC, and therefore that such problems must be regarded as semi-permanent. Tecsiel found that congestion problems, when experienced, tended to last for several hours – this should obviously be taken into account if/when the application prototype is being demonstrated.

3.8 Recommendations Concerning the Application Prototype

A throughput of 3 Kbit/s leads to an estimate for the turnaround of a transaction of 1 minute rather than the 5 – 15 seconds hoped for. The expectations for the application prototype were consequently amended.

It is believed that all the sites that participated in the tests can expect to participate in the application prototype with reasonable success. For demonstrations to those outside the project, results are more likely to be successful between France and Germany than between other countries. (This assumes that the present conditions obtain when demonstrations take place.)

4 Standardization Activities

4.1 Standards

The main objective of the standardization work has been to foster and direct the participation by the majority of the project's partners in national and international standards activities and work programmes. All of the partners active in this task have a history of ongoing participation in standardization activities (either for graphics or for networking) at the national level and, for most, at the international level as well. This task's activity has provided an independent mechanism for discussion of standards issues and enabled the formation of a harmonized European view on a number of these issues.

ARGOSI's involvement in the standardization process has been directed by the overall aims of the project, namely, to further the integration of graphics and networking standards, as well as pursuing specific standards projects where individuals have particular expertise and involvement. In some cases, this has led to the initiation and/or support of new work items within the international arena, for example, the CGM/FTAM document type and the X/OSI mapping. In other cases, individual expertise made available through the support of ARGOSI has meant that existing ISO/IEC projects have been seen through to completion within the schedules agreed for those projects (for example, the Computer Graphics Interface project and the SC24 study group on User Requirements). It could be argued that, in at least one case, this would not have been possible if ARGOSI support had not been available.

ARGOSI individuals have also held significant international positions as convenors and document editors. Specifically, the SC24/WG3 Convenorship was held by D.B. Arnold and later by A. Ducrot. Document editors include P. Artico, R.A. Day, D.A. Duce and G.J. Reynolds.

ARGOSI's involvement in standards has also been bounded by ISO/IEC procedures which require that all contributions come through the national standards organizations of the participating members of its sub-committees. Thus, contributions that ARGOSI has prepared have had to obtain approval through one or more national bodies.

The main contributions made by ARGOSI in specific standards areas are described below.

- ISO/IEC 9636 – Computer graphics – Interfacing techniques for dialogues with computer graphics devices (CGI) Functional specification (Parts 1 – 6), edited by G.J. Reynolds. ARGOSI has supported the development of this standard from DIS (draft international standard) through to IS (international standard) by providing funding for the document editor and issues librarian (R. Fairbairns).
- EWOS Technical guide 013. A mapping of the X window system over an OSI stack (May 1991), edited by R.A. Day. ARGOSI has supported the development of this technical guide from its inception and has played a substantial part in its progress. The development of an OSI mapping for the X window system data stream protocol is seen as essential to the use of X in Europe if X becomes a European standard at some future date. In America, the ANSC X3H3 committee standardising the data stream protocol added a part 4 to the draft standard using EWOS TG 013.
- FTAM Constraint Set and Document Type for CGM – version 1.6, September 1991, edited by E. Pelucchi and P. Artico. The development of this document type for FTAM is a direct requirement from the ARGOSI demonstrator. It is also one of the first structured file access document types to be registered. The document has been submitted to EWOS and accepted as addendum 3 to the DISP (Draft International Standardized Profile) for FTAM. Tecsiel plan to continue supporting this work after the end of the ARGOSI project, by providing the document editor (P. Artico).
- User requirements survey and report, edited by L. Frobose. A report relating the ISO/IEC JTC1/SC24 User Requirements survey to the data collected for the ARGOSI classification task. The SC24 survey was initiated before this project started and has been actively supported by FhG (being one of the two principal researchers). Comparison between this survey and the ARGOSI classification survey results has shown similar interpretation of the results, where comparison was appropriate.

Other contributions and activities that have been supported by ARGOSI include:

- CGM/ASN.1 study: The study of services work on an ASN.1 description of basic CGM, which is needed for integrating CGMs in ODA documents (for example) has been input to ISO/IEC JTC1/SC24 for consideration. Whilst this work will not have reached a stage, by the end of this project, where a new work item could have been initiated, it will form a substantial part of an initial draft for such a work item. It is hoped that this work will begin as an ISO project following the SC24 meeting in October 1992. (Note that a number of the ARGOSI partners are interested in pursuing this work beyond the project's timescale.)

- ARGOSI classification report: Circulated to both ISO/IEC JTC1 SC24 and SC21 as a discussion document.
- CGM amendments: ARGOSI contributions on Amendments 1 and 3 have been submitted via national standards organizations as comments on the relevant letter ballots. ARGOSI partners have also participated at the appropriate CGM editing/ rapporteur group meetings.
- Application profiles: following on from the recommendations on application profiles from the Breuberg workshop (see below) a position paper on ISP's for graphics was distributed to SC24. The proposed Amendment 4 to the CGM (concerned with application profiles) has been reviewed and comments have been produced.
- Computer graphics reference model: this project has had support from a few of the ARGOSI partners. While not being directly related to the other aspects of this project, the CGRM is intended to have a controlling influence on future graphics standards which may incorporate a stronger link between graphics and networking.
- GKS revision: RAL have been active in this project through the provision of the document editors. Other ARGOSI partners have attended editing meetings or provided input papers to this project.
- New API (PREMO): FhG have been active in the study group and the formulation of the new work item proposal for this project. ARGOSI funding has been used to support their involvement. RAL also contributed to this work. The study group have taken a rather wide view of what functionality is to be considered, and have included areas such as multi-media and windowing systems, both of which have strong links with distributed processing and networking.
- Participation at national standards meetings: ARGOSI partners have participated in the following national standards committees during the project: BSI IST/31 & IST/21 (United Kingdom), AFNOR CN24 (France), DIN/SC24 & SC21 (Germany), and UNINFO (Italy). In addition, ANSC X3H3 (USA) meetings were attended by two of the project's partners as international observers.
- Participation at international meetings: ISO/IEC and EWOS: ARGOSI partners have participated in the following international standards committees during the project:
  - ISO/IEC JTC1/SC24 including working groups (1 – 5),
  - ISO/IEC JTC1/SC21 including working groups (5 – 7),
  - ISO/IEC JTC1/SC2, EWOS including TA & EGFT.

4.2 CGM and FTAM

4.2.1 Introduction

ARGOSI recognized the need for effective access to bulk graphical data over OSI networks. Specifically, as a result of studies on a range of distributed graphics applications (see Chap. 2), it identified the Computer Graphics Metafile (CGM),[1] a standard format for the storage and later display of two-dimensional pictures, as a data structure that needs to be manipulated across an OSI network by a certain class of such applications. In an OSI environment the natural choice to do this is File Transfer, Access and Management (FTAM).[2] However, existing FTAM implementations were able only to access a CGM as an unstructured binary file – i.e. to transfer the whole file, with no ability to access the inherent structure within.

In many cases the distributed graphics applications studied by ARGOSI are required to work over low-bandwidth networks. Therefore efficient use of the bandwidth available is required, and consequently the ability to transfer only those parts of the CGM that are needed by the application. The project therefore decided to develop the ability for FTAM to be able to access the structure within a CGM. To do this it was necessary to develop a suitable FTAM 'document type'. This document type was then implemented within the three different FTAM implementations of interest to the project. The implementation was done in the context of the ARGOSI demonstrator (see Chap. 5) which brought together this aspect of the integration of graphics and OSI standards, along with a number of other issues.

4.2.2 Mapping the CGM onto FTAM

To understand how the CGM structure was mapped onto the FTAM service it is first necessary to explain the structural concepts of the CGM. The CGM standard provides a format for capturing 2D static pictures. The format consists of an ordered set of elements, which have a hierarchical structure as shown in Fig. 4.1. At the top level it consists of a 'metafile descriptor' (MFD) which contains information pertaining to the CGM as a whole (including a name for the CGM), followed by a series of independent pictures. At the next level each individual picture is described, in terms of a 'picture descriptor' which contains information pertaining to the picture (again, including a name), followed by the 'picture body'. Finally, there is a level giving the structure of the picture itself – some control information plus the series of lines, markers and other graphical information that constitute the picture. At each of the levels there are delimiter elements that mark the beginning and end of the relevant structures – BM (begin metafile) and EM (end metafile) at the metafile level, BP (begin picture) and EP (end picture) at the picture level, and BPB (begin picture body) within the picture to mark where the actual picture itself starts.

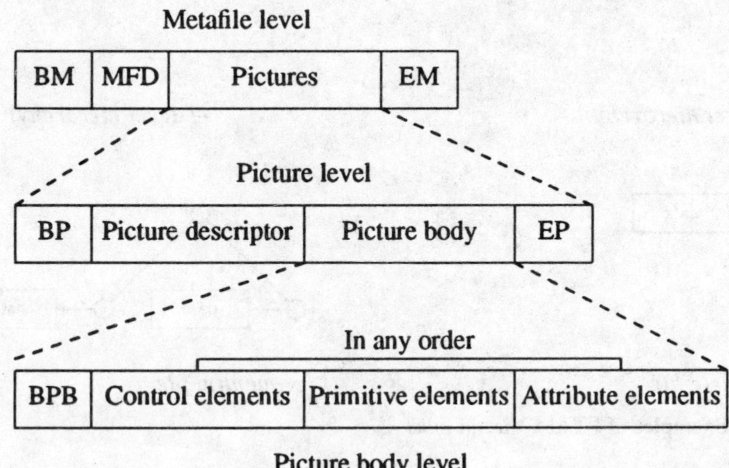

Fig. 4.1. Structure of the Computer Graphics Metafile

Besides defining the structure of the CGM, the standard also defines three different sets of encoding rules with which to encode the information in a real file: a 'character' encoding, a 'binary' encoding and a 'clear text' encoding. These each have different characteristics concerning the ease of generation and interpretation, size of the resulting metafile and ease of transmission between systems.

FTAM provides a service for the reading and writing of entire files, or of parts of individual files, as well as some file management services. The standard allows access to the structure within an individual file, provided that the structure can be represented within the FTAM model of a filestore. As the ways in which real filestores are implemented vary considerably between existing systems, a common model for describing files and their attributes is needed before FTAM service elements can be defined in an OSI environment. Such a model is provided by the FTAM 'virtual filestore'.

Within the virtual filestore, FTAM defines a virtual file as an 'unambiguously named collection of structured information having a common set of attributes'. The basic access units of a file and their relationships are described by the file access structure. This is a tree structure that describes the file in terms of the units which can be accessed separately (FADUs – File Access Data Units). Note that the virtual filestore tree is a way of representing structure in an individual file and *not* modelling a whole hierarchical filestore, such as a Unix filesystem.

A FADU is the minimal access unit and is a subtree of the hierarchical file; the actual data units are associated with the nodes of the tree, and can be identified through FTAM either by their relative order within the file or by name (where there is a suitable naming structure defined in the real file represented). When a file is represented as a single level hierarchy, access is possible only to the file as a whole. When it is represented as a multiple level hierarchy, access is possible to individual elements (e.g. individual records within a file). This is illustrated in Fig. 4.2.

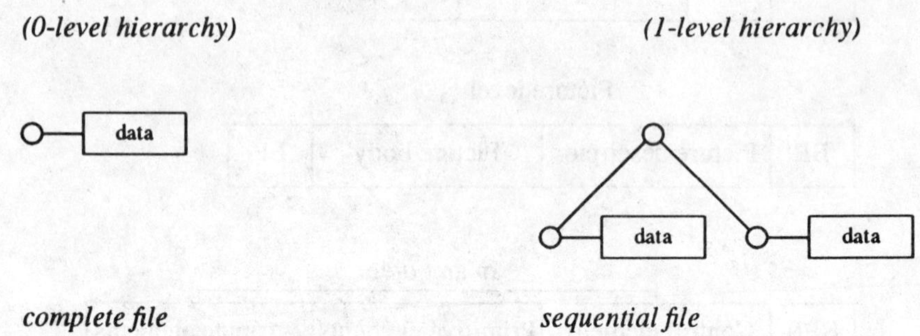

Fig. 4.2. Examples of FTAM Virtual Files

FTAM introduces the idea of a set of 'document types' each of which define for a specific type of file the constraints on the file structure, the data types forming the data units and how the structure of a real file maps onto the FTAM virtual filestore. The ARGOSI project created a new FTAM document type to allow structured access to the CGM.

To create the new document type a mapping of the CGM onto the FTAM virtual filestore was required. This meant that a number of choices had to be made. The first of these was to decide the level of access required. It was decided to allow access to the level of an individual picture, but (at this stage) not to attempt access to the structures within a picture. The second choice was to decide what were the sequences of FADUs that were likely to be transferred. It was decided that the most common scenarios would be to transfer either a single picture, a series of pictures, or the metafile descriptor (possibly with one or more pictures). Furthermore, in the case where a physical file in a remote filestore contains more than one complete CGM, the ability to transfer one or more CGMs from within an entire file might be wanted.

These considerations led to the mapping shown in Fig. 4.3. This example shows the mapping of a single physical file containing two CGMs. The first 'metal' contains a single picture; the second 'meta2' contains two pictures. By mapping each picture as a separate FADU at level 2 (i.e. complete with its deliminating BP and EP elements) these can each be accessed independently. Similary the metafile descriptor (MFD) is mapped to a separate FADU and can be accessed independently as well. Finally, each CGM within the file can be accessed at level 1 as a separate FADU.

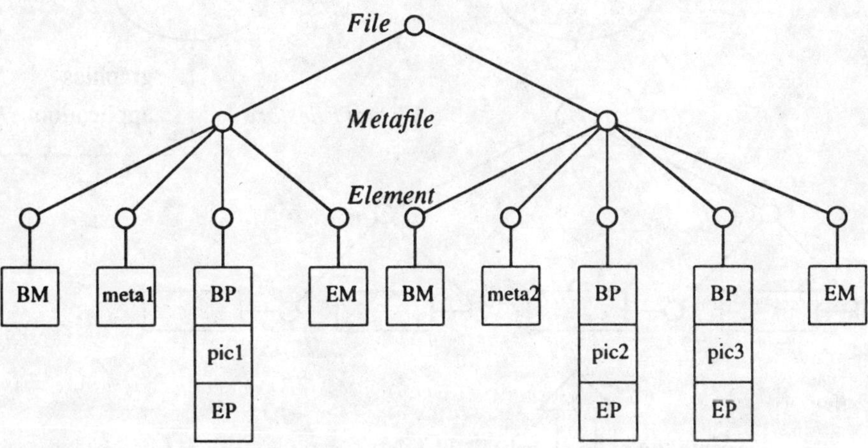

Fig. 4.3. Mapping of CGM onto FTAM Virtual Filestore

In order to be able to access these FADUs by name, the names contained within the CGM to identify the metafile and pictures are used. Thus the level 1 FADU representing the first metafile in Fig. 4.3 is named by FTAM as *meta1* , the picture is named *pic1* and the other level 2 FADUs, corresponding to elements that have no names contained within them are named conventionally as *meta1.bm*, *meta1.mfd* and *meta1.em*. This naming allows the FTAM user (or distributed graphics application) to select individual metafiles and pictures by the names relevant within the graphics domain.

4.2.3 Implementation of the Document Type

To implement the document type it was necessary to make modifications to the FTAM implementation in use. These modifications centred mainly around the FTAM responder, which is the entity that maps a request (such as F-READ) made by a distributed graphics application (acting as the FTAM initiator) onto the real filestore which contains the CGM. To do this it must be able to determine that the file being accessed is a CGM, and be able to parse the file in sufficient detail that it can locate those elements of the total structure that are required. The relationship between the FTAM initiator, responder and the real filestore is depicted in Fig. 4.4.

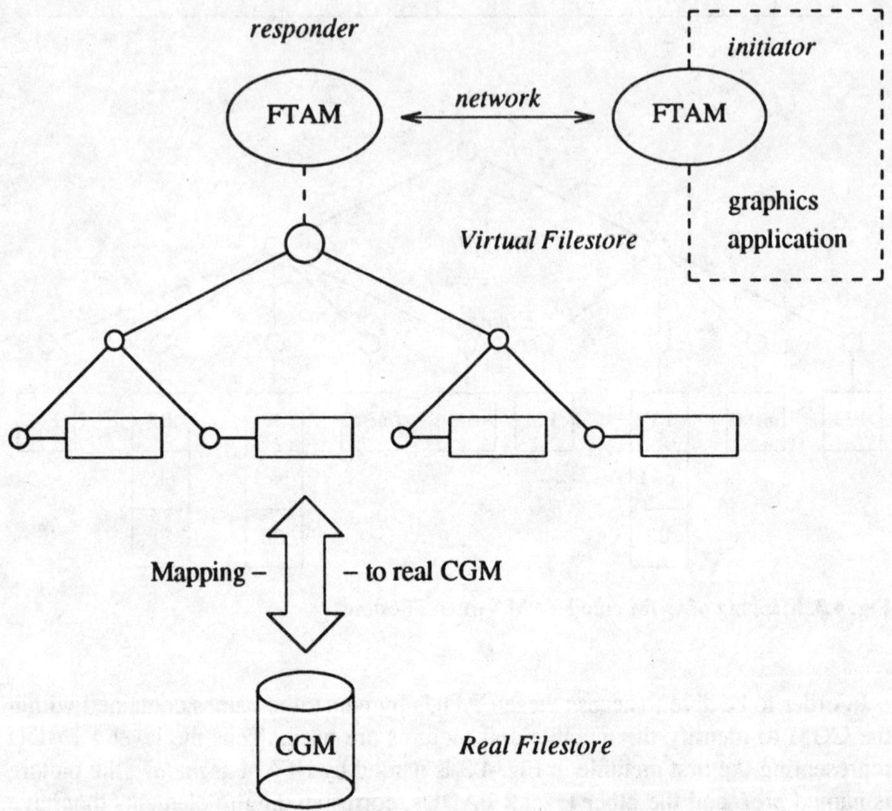

Fig. 4.4. Relationships Between Application and FTAM Components

It is important to note that this last operation will in practice have to be done by the FTAM responder itself, rather than by the underlying operating system. This is because the latter generally will not have support for structured access to a complex object like the CGM. Contrast this with the support often found within an operating system for simpler file structures, such as indexed sequential files. Although it is clearly possible in principle that a file such as a CGM could be represented in the real filestore in a way that allowed the operating system to support structured access – perhaps as a file with each picture as a separate logical record – current graphics software does not do this. Such files are invariably written as text or binary data with little or no correlation between CGM structure and any record structure within the underlying file structure. Indeed, it is unlikely that the operating system will be aware that a specific file within its filestore is a CGM, so this fact will also need to be determined by the FTAM responder.

Therefore the implementation involved writing a simple CGM parser for incorporation into each of the FTAM responders used within the project. To give access down to picture level is relatively simple, and a small finite state machine was written into each. This gave each responder the ability to form a mapping table which related the various structural elements within the CGM to their byte offsets within the physical file. From this table it could then extract the element(s) required by a FTAM initiator's request.

The FTAM implementations upgraded in this way by the project were:

- the Tecsiel X/FT FTAM product;
- the FTAM product used by Thomson-CSF in a number of its systems (based on a Marben implementation);
- the ISODE FTAM (at versions 6.0 and 7.0 of ISODE).

Implementing the CGM document type requires an ability to handle 'two levels depth hierarchical' mappings of files. The Tecsiel and Marben implementations already had support for this but it was necessary to add this to the ISODE implementation. The resources available to the project meant that it was not possible to implement the entire functionality of the CGM document type that was developed. It was therefore decided to provide support only for reading parts of a CGM (and not for writing), and to limit reading to FTAM UA (unstructured all) 'access context' – i.e. so that only the entire contents of a FADU are transferred, without the possibility of transferring individual level $n+1$ FADUs within a level n FADU. In practice these are reasonable limitations, and of course the document type as defined by the project allows a fuller range of functionality.

It was decided also to support only one form of encoding of the CGM as defined in the standard – the 'binary' encoding. The project believes that this is the only encoding that is guaranteed to work over an OSI network,[4] although the document type as defined also allows access to a CGM encoded using the 'character' encoding of the CGM standard.

The document type defined by ARGOSI has been submitted to EWOS[5] for standardization as a registered document type within ISO/IEC.

4.2.4 Evaluation of Document Types for General Structured Access

The CGM document type was successfully implemented in all three FTAM implementations, and all interworked with each other. The FTAM products were used within the ARGOSI demonstration shown at the Esprit '91 Exhibition, where their use was shown in accessing graphical information in Brussels from sites in the UK, France, Germany and Italy (using each of these countries' public data networks).

Thus the use of a FTAM document type to map the CGM structure has proven to be a valid means of achieving structured access to this type of graphical information in an OSI environment. It is useful, however, to consider the general applicability of the method, based on the lessons learnt in this project.

The first point is that, as the FTAM virtual filestore is a hierarchical structure, mapping a non-hierarchical object onto it may be difficult. The CGM is hierarchical, and consequently did not present too many problems, although a considerable amount of thought was needed to determine where to place the elements of the CGM in the virtual filestore. If this is not done carefully the required access may be difficult or impossible to achieve.

An important lesson of the project was that the ability to understand enough of the CGM to provide structured access had to be placed in the FTAM responder (refer to Fig. 4.4). Normally this will not be part of the graphics application that requires access to the CGM (as this latter will usually contain the FTAM initiator in a distributed application environment). Unfortunately it is the graphics application that is able to parse the CGM, so this functionality is actually being duplicated in the responder. In the present case this was not a major issue, but it should be noted that if the ability to access a CGM encoded using the character encoding as well as the binary encoding had been needed the parser code would have had to have been duplicated (in order to recognize CGM elements in either encoding). Furthermore, if access had been required to deeper levels (e.g. within an individual picture), a much more complex parser would have been needed – this would probably have been non-trivial to implement. Additionally, a general-purpose FTAM implementation will become increasingly complex as support for further document types of this sort is added in future.

Thus the use of the document type seems to be a technique that is useful provided that the work of implementing the mapping between virtual and real filestore within the responder is straightforward. It is interesting to speculate as to whether there are alternatives to the general method. One possibility would be to adopt the 'fileserving' paradigm, for example as implemented by the NFS.[3] In such a case the graphics application might then be able to 'see' a remote CGM as a simple series of bytes (assuming that the implementation of the remote filesystem allowed such a representation across the network). It could then use its own knowledge of what the structure of a CGM is, in exactly the same way as it would do when accessing a CGM stored locally.

However, such a scenario may not be as simple as it seems at first sight. Apart from the problem of representing a file across a network (which is a similar problem in the fileserving paradigm to that addressed by the virtual filestore in FTAM), there is also the problem of ensuring efficient bandwidth usage. If the application needs to read 90 percent of a remote CGM to find the picture that it requires (because the picture is at the end of the CGM), a large amount of unwanted information will still be transmitted in the search alone.

It may be that a more general solution of this class of problem requires an extension of the document type model within FTAM. For example, there may be a need for sufficient functionality within the FTAM service that a document type that treats a remote file as a flat byte stream can be used, in conjunction with a suitable service primitive that allows the initiator to request the responder to search for a specified part of the file contents before transferring it. This would then allow the initiator to retain the detailed, application-specific knowledge of the structure being accessed, whilst allowing the responder to find the required part of the file without incurring network traffic before the actual transfer of the wanted information.

4.3 ASN.1 Notation for CGM

4.3.1 Background and Overview

One of the recommendations of the Breuberg Workshop (see Chap. 6) was that ARGOSI should develop an ASN.1 encoding for CGM. ASN.1 is a notation for describing structured information, typically for transmission across a network, standardized by ISO/IEC and CCITT. ASN.1 separates the issue of describing the structure of information, from the issue of how that information is to be represented for transmission. Given an ASN.1 description of a message, a representation can be derived mechanically by applying a set of encoding rules. Such a set of rules, known as the Basic Encoding Rules (BER), has also been standardized. ASN.1 and the Basic Encoding Rules are ISO standards 8824:1987 and 8825:1987 respectively. They continue to be developed collaboratively by ISO/IEC and CCITT. At the present time, CCITT have published agreed revisions to the 1987 ISO standards (Recommendations X.208 and X.209, 1989), but the corresponding ISO documents are still in the publication process.

The requirement for ASN.1 specification of CGM is seen as twofold: a requirement for a means of *notation* and a requirement for a means of *encoding* CGMs derived from this notation. It is essential that the distinction between notation and encoding is borne in mind.

The requirements for a means of *notation* that are satisfied by ASN.1 are as follows.

- There is a need for an unambiguous syntactic description of the CGM data structures in a form that is standardized. ASN.1 fulfills this need by providing a notation that is comprehensible to non-experts, as well as providing enough rigour to minimize ambiguity. Note that ASN.1 does not attempt to solve the problems of formal specification and/or proof of semantic correctness of the CGM specification in the sense that expression in a language such as LOTOS might. This is not the intention of this work.

- To interact effectively with OSI standards, there is a need to have a notation which can be registered as an "abstract syntax" for OSI use. This means that it will then be possible for OSI application services to reference it, and hence to "understand" the structure of the CGM. Some examples of this are as follows:
  - a FTAM document type could reference the abstract syntax to provide access to the structure of the CGM (see below for more detail on this);
  - MHS could reference the abstract syntax as a defined body part, and hence an implementation of a mail user interface could recognize a CGM included as part of a mail message and invoke an interpreter to display the graphical output;
  - ODA could reference the abstract syntax in a similar way to include a CGM in a document.

  Note that the last two examples (MHS and ODA) may well not require structured access to the CGM, and therefore could be accomplished without a knowledge of the CGM abstract syntax. (ODA already has the concept of inclusion of the CGM, essentially as a "black box" within an ODA document.) However, there is merit in providing a uniform method of treating the CGM in OSI applications, as well as an element of future-proofing.

The requirements for a means of *encoding* that are satisfied by ASN.1 are as follows.

- Tools exist to process ASN.1 notations and to produce code in a programming language (usually C). This code allows a programmer to produce a program that will encode instances of data structures, the abstract syntaxes of which have been expressed in ASN.1, in the standardized Basic Encoding Rules, and subsequently to decode the BER encoded form. Thus it would be possible with a minimum of effort to construct the encoding part of a CGM generator, and the corresponding decoder part of an interpreter. The fact that this was being done using automatic tools would give a high degree of confidence that the encoding and decoding processes were being carried out correctly.
- Part of the encoding and decoding processes can include the automatic checking of some elements of the CGM being processed (e.g. that values of parameters are consistent with ranges specified in the ASN.1 notation), but it is not clear how useful this would be. Note that more sophisticated checking of semantics (e.g. the optimization of redundant elements) would not come as part of the use of these tools, but that some simple checking, such as that for legal ordering of elements, should be possible.

The work undertaken in ARGOSI had several goals.

- To develop an ASN.1 notation for the CGM including Amendment 1. It is also the intention to explore Amendment 3 if this is available in a stable form within the timescales of the ARGOSI work.

- To develop a prototype encoder and decoder using ASN.1 tools in order to:
  - demonstrate the feasibility of encoding real CGMs into BER and their subsequent decoding;
  - investigate the usefulness of existing tools in aiding the implementation process;
  - investigate the suitability or otherwise of the BER as an encoding method.

  A prototype was produced using an ASN.1 notation of a cut-down version of the CGM specification (see Appendix 3). The methodology employed was to produce an encoder that read a clear-text encoded CGM in order to populate the C language data structures produced by use of the ISODE ASN.1 tools with the notation shown in Appendix 3. These data structures are then encoded into a BER representation of the CGM, using an encoder routine also generated by the ASN.1 tools. A corresponding decoder uses an automatically generated decoder to translate the BER back to C language data structures, which are then "printed out" in clear-text form. Thus the prototype effectively produced two tools – one to translate a clear-text encoded CGM into BER, and one to perform the opposite translation.
- To demonstrate the use of the notation in implementing the document type EWOS-1 (i.e. the document type developed to allow access to the picture structure of the CGM – previously known as the FTAM-6 document type) in FTAM.

4.3.2 Coverage of CGM Elements

The ARGOSI work has developed an ASN.1 description for a substantial subset of the CGM elements. The work started by concentrating on the major structuring and control elements of ISO 8632:1987, a single graphical element, polyline and its associated attribute elements. Having established a basic style for writing the description, the subset was extended to include other graphical elements and their attributes. At the time of writing, an ASN.1 description exists for all the CGM graphical elements and attributes, apart from text, restricted text and GDP, and for all elements of other categories apart from:

Integer Precision
Real Precision
Index Precision
Colour Precision
Colour Index Precision
VDC Integer Precision
VDC Real Precision
Escape
Message
Application Data

Incorporating the text elements does not cause any difficulty at the syntactic level, the difficulty is at the semantic level. It is not clear which ASN.1 datatype should be used to represent characters. This is an area of ASN.1 which is under revision within ISO/CCITT to provide closer harmonization with the work of other committees, and requires further thought.

The precision elements pose a different problem. These elements are optional within CGM and their meanings, if present, are encoding dependent. With the ASN.1 Basic Encoding Rules (BER) it is not clear how the precision elements could be used and what meaning could be given to them because the encoding technique automatically produces the most compact encoding for types such as integer, taking into account the value to be encoded. However, the precision elements are used by some systems to pass information between a CGM generator and CGM interpreter, so that an interpreter can adapt itself to the precision of a particular metafile. The datatype used to describe precision is different in each of the three standardized encodings; it may be that the solution is to allow the ASN.1 notation to accept any of these forms. However, the implications require wider discussion before a decision is reached.

4.3.3 Approach to ASN.1 Description

The ASN.1 description of the CGM subset follows almost exactly the structure of the formal grammar (which is expressed in a BNF notation) in Annex A of CGM, with some minor flattening of the structure in places. Data types used in the CGM description map well onto the data types and type constructors of ASN.1. The SEQUENCE constructor is used in ASN.1 to describe types which are tuples of other types (for example RGB consists of three reals representing red, green and blue components) and also to represent CGM list types.

The distinction between real and integer VDC values is made at a higher level in the ASN.1 description than in CGM Annex A. The type is associated with a structured value such as a point list rather than with individual points.

4.3.4 ARGOSI CGM-ASN.1 Tools

A software module has been developed which generates and interprets BER encoded metafiles. The approach taken has been to develop an interface between the GMD toolkit and a new ASN encoder module generated from the POSY/PEPY ASN.1 tools in ISODE. Essentially this is an ASN.1 backend to the CGM generator. The GMD toolkit provides a programming language interface and parameter checking. The interface between the CGM toolkit and the ASN module is a text file that is a Clear Text encoded CGM metafile. The full generality of the clear text encoding is not necessary for this purpose and the format used is a profile of the full encoding.

The Generator. The generator consists of a parser that recognizes the elements in the CGM profile used. C functions are called (one for each CGM element) to create an instance of a C data structure that represents the metafile to be encoded. The general form of the data structures is automatically created by the ASN.1 tools, from the ASN.1 CGM notation. The encode function (also generated automatically by the ASN.1 tools) is then called to generate the transfer syntax of the metafile, by applying the BERs to the instance of the data structure.

The Unix(TM) *lex* tool has been used to generate the parser from a specification of the CGM clear text profile used.

The Interpreter. The interpreter generates a textual representation of the BER encoded metafile. In ASN.1 terminology, this corresponds to the ASN.1 value notation of the ASN.1 type representing the metafile. The textual representation adopted corresponds to the Clear Text encoding notation. The interpreter is based on a pretty printer routine which is automatically generated by the ISODE ASN.1 tools. The output from this routine is transformed by a module generated with *lex*, to produce the clear text notation elements.

4.3.5 Comparison of BER with Other Encodings

The size of BER metafile encodings were compared to the size of encodings generated by the binary or character schemes specified in ISO/IEC 8632. The comparison work is based on a set of 52 metafiles generated in the ARGOSI project and 28 metafiles from the NCGA set of test metafiles.

The ARGOSI metafiles are derived from the ARGOSI demonstrator application (see Chap. 5). One set of 28 metafiles contains information about country boundaries for different resolutions of a map of Europe. This set just uses polygon and fill index graphical elements. A second set of 21 metafiles contains road information for parts of Europe. They contain line index and line elements. Size and element distributions for each of the metafiles have been computed.

The NCGA set consists of metafiles representing a wide range of applications (including simple business graphics, CAD, architecture, geographics, robotics and art); these were used at the NCGA'89 CGM interchange demonstration.

The translation from binary to character and clear text encodings was carried out using the GMD CGM toolkit. BER encodings of the metafiles have been generated using the tools described in the previous section.

4.3.6 Final Status

By the end of the project, initial comparison data for the ARGOSI and NCGA metafiles had been obtained. The NCGA metafiles had to be modified to remove the types of elements (mainly text elements) not supported by the ARGOSI BER tool. The same changes were also made to the binary and character representations of these metafiles.

More work is necessary in order to fully understand what is happening in the different encodings, and in particular what effects are intrinsic properties of the individual methods and what are artifacts of the tools used to generate the encodings. However, evidence is growing to support some initial findings.

4.3.7 Interim Conclusions

Efficiency of BER Encodings. The ARGOSI map metafiles containing polygon elements differ only in the number of polygon elements and the number of vertices per polygon. The sizes of the BER and character encodings compared to the size of the binary encoding for each of these metafiles are shown in Table 4.1 below. Comparisons are made against the binary encoding because, as noted earlier, the ARGOSI project holds the opinion that only the binary encoding is suitable for use in the OSI environment. The character encodings of these files are roughly 0.8 times the size of the binary encodings. The BER encodings are consistently close to 2.5 times the size of the binary encodings. The files all use integer VDC type. The ISODE ASN.1 tools correctly implement the BER method for encoding integers.

The reason for the size inefficiency of the BER encoded metafiles is due to the tag, length, value coding technique which is fundamental to BER. The structure of the BER encoding for a data value is shown in Fig. 4.5. The identifier octets encode the ASN.1 tag of the type of the data value, the length octets specify the number of octets in the contents octets and the contents octets encode the data value.

First consider the encoding of an integer value. This requires one octet for the identifier, and one for the length. The contents field is of variable length, having a size of 1 octet if the integer is in the range −128..127, 2 octets for −32768..32767 etc. Typically 1+1+2 octets are required for each coordinate.

A point with INTEGER VDCTYPE is described in ASN.1 as:

```
IntegerPoint ::= SEQUENCE {
  x-coordinate                    [0] INTEGER,
  y-coordinate                    [1] INTEGER }
```

A point is encoded as an identifier, length, and value, where the value consists of the encodings for the two coordinates. Thus a point typically requires 10 octets. A list of points is encoded as identifier and length followed by the encoding of each of the points in the list. For metafiles containing frequent occurrences of short lists the extra identifier and length are a significant overhead; for metafiles containing small numbers of long lists, they are less so. This situation is to be compared to the binary encoding where a point typically requires 4 octets and the overall element length is 4 times the number of points plus a 4 octet header.

Table 4.1. Comparison of Sizes for ARGOSI Map Metafiles

Metafile Name	BER/binary	Character/binary
a_pic11	2.49	0.79
a_pic12	2.48	0.77
a_pic13	2.46	0.82
a_pic14	2.49	0.78
a_pic15	2.48	0.75
a_pic16	2.47	0.78
a_pic17	2.48	0.76
a_pic18	2.48	0.75
a_pic19	2.49	0.77
a_pic1a	2.47	0.81
a_pic1b	2.46	0.79
a_pic1c	2.47	0.81
a_pic1d	2.47	0.82
a_pic1e	2.48	0.80
a_pic1f	2.48	0.81
a_pic1g	2.45	0.79
a_pic21	2.48	0.86
a_pic22	2.47	0.83
a_pic23	2.45	0.88
a_pic24	2.47	0.87
a_pic25	2.49	0.82
a_pic26	2.47	0.86
a_pic27	2.47	0.85
a_pic28	2.47	0.88
a_pic29	2.46	0.89
a_pic2a	2.47	0.89
a_pic2b	2.42	0.87
a_pict3	2.46	0.86

Identifier Octets	Length Octets	Contents Octets

Fig. 4.5. Structure of a BER Encoding

The inefficiency in the BER encoding stems from the inclusion of identifier and length fields on every coordinate and every point. The identifier fields on points are certainly redundant in the sense that every point has the same type.

For the encoding of reals, the situation is more complicated. In the ISODE ASN.1 tool, the local representation of reals uses the C 'double' type. There is no way to limit the precision when a BER encoding is generated with the result that a real point requires 22 octets using the ISODE tool.

There is also the extra overhead of the structured types used in the ASN.1 notation to take into account. As an example, consider the notation for the POLYLINE element. This has been expressed in ASN.1 as follows (assuming INTEGER VDCTYPE):

```
GraphicalElement ::= CHOICE {
   polyline            [0] Pointlist,
                             .
                             .
                       }

PointList          ::= CHOICE {
   integerPointList    [0] SEQUENCE SIZE (1..MAX) OF IntegerPoint,
                             .
                             .
                       }

IntegerPoint       ::= SEQUENCE {
   x-coordinate        [0] INTEGER,
   y-coordinate        [1] INTEGER
                       }
```

Consider further that a POLYLINE of three points *<x1,y1>* , *<x2,y2>* , *<x3,y3>* (each of which can be expressed as 16-bit integers) must be encoded. Using the ASN.1 notation and the BER gives the following encoding, with a total length for the POLYLINE of 34 bytes, as shown in Fig. 4.6. (Note: the octet contents are represented in hexadecimal.) In contrast, the binary encoding is much more compact. The equivalent POLYLINE has a total length of 14 bytes, as shown in Fig. 4.7.

Thus it can be seen that, in this example, the ratio (BER/binary) of encoding lengths is 2.43. So the number of points in the POLYLINE (or similar) element increases the influence of the structure headers becomes less marked, and the ratio will be determined by the difference in encoding lengths for the integer point pairs (i.e. 2.50). This corresponds with the experimental results shown in Table 4.1.

It is clear that there is a size efficiency problem. The ASN.1 BERs do not appear to be rich enough to circumvent this limitation, without following the unacceptable path of introducing application dependent encoding techniques for entities such as point lists and presenting these with the ASN.1 octet string type.

In principle there is enough information in the ASN.1 type for the encoding generator to apply some optimizations if the encoding rules allowed this, for example to factor out tags on structures of items of the same type. However, this would certainly violate the fundamental principles of the BERs and requires

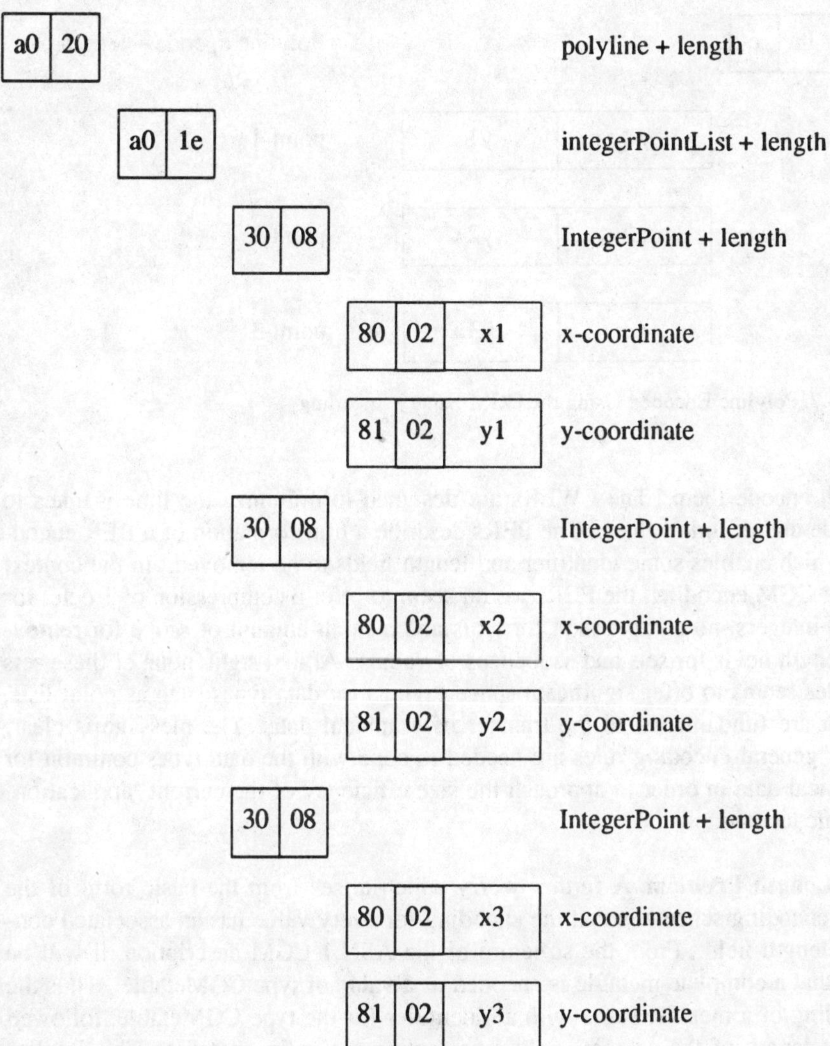

Fig. 4.6. Polyline Encoded Using the BER

careful thought. There is a clear need for discussion with the originators of ASN.1 and the encoding rules to correctly identify the problem and understand what options are available for its solution.

There are three further sets of encoding rules under development within SC21, the Packed Encoding Rules (PER), Light Weight Encoding Rules (LWER) and Distinguished Encoding Rules (DER). The DERs are designed for use where a one to one correspondence is required between the values and the octet strings

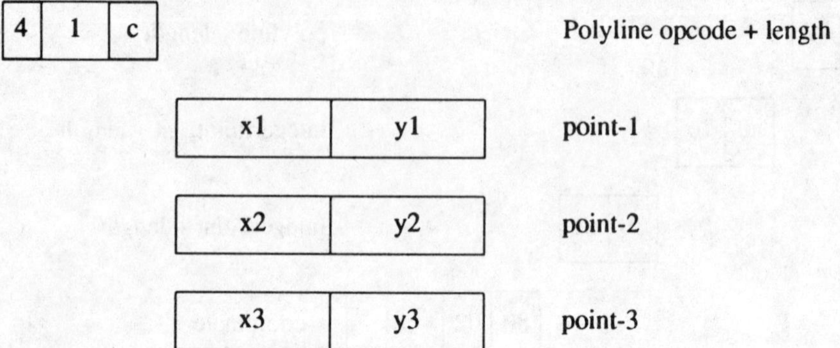

Fig. 4.7. Polyline Encoded Using the CGM Binary Encoding

which encode them. The LWERs are designed to minimize the time it takes to encode and decode values. The PERs describe a transformation of a BER encoding which enables some identifier and length fields to be removed. In the context of the CGM encoding, the PERs would seem to offer a compression of 1 octet for small integers, no compression for reals and a small amount of scope for removing length fields for sets and sequences of values. At first sight, none of these sets of rules seems to offer significant space savings for data types such as point lists, which are fundamental to the transfer of graphical data. The message is clear: better general encoding rules are needed to cope with the data types common for graphical data in order to approach the size efficiency of the current 'application' specific techniques.

The Length Problem. A further worry which arises from the basic form of the BER encoding scheme is that the encoding for every value has an associated contents length field. From the structure of the ASN.1 CGM description, it will be seen that a complete metafile is encoded as a value of type CGMetafile. Thus the encoding of a metafile starts with an identifier for the type CGMetafile, followed by the length of the contents field representing the entire metafile. This implies that the complete metafile has to be stored before the first octets of the encoding can be generated. The BERs do allow an alternative encoding structure shown in Fig. 4.8, in which the length octets are replaced by a distinguished value which indicates that the contents octets are terminated by an end of contents marker but this merely serves to move the problem from the transmitter to the receiver.

Identifier Octets	Indefinite Length Octets	Contents Octets	End of Contents Octets

Fig. 4.8. Structure of a BER Encoding

4.4 Mapping of the X Window System onto an OSI stack

ANSI, the US national standards body, has been working for some time on the creation of a national standard based on the X Window System. It is their intention to submit the national standard to ISO/IEC for 'fast track' standardization. To do this requires the development of an internationally acceptable mapping of X Windows over an OSI network; at present mappings only exist for TCP/IP and DECnet networks.

X Windows provides a windowing system based on the client/server model, and this model can be extended across a network. This is illustrated in Fig. 4.9.

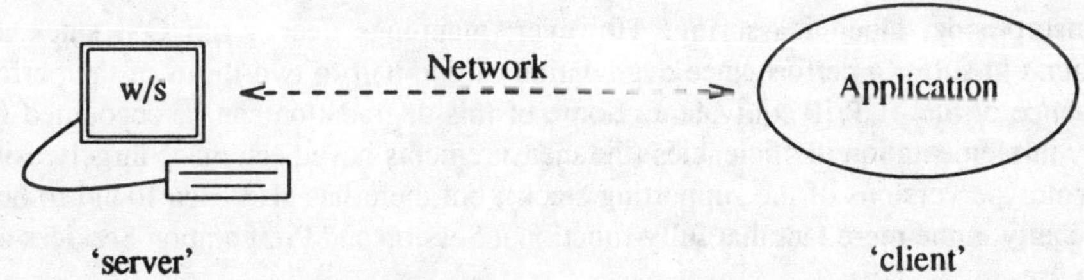

Fig. 4.9. Client/server Architecture of X Windows

The specification of X Windows asks only for a 'reliable byte stream' to be provided to do this. This is usually interpreted as a mapping at the Transport Service level. If an attempt is made to map X Windows over a full OSI stack an immediate problem is encountered in that the full stack provides more data-management services than are required by X Windows. Many of these services are either not required, or are already provided by the X Windows *byte stream protocol*. The extent of this overlap is shown in Fig. 4.10.

A number of developers have already attempted a mapping of X Windows over the full OSI stack, and over a partial stack extending up to the Transport Layer. Performance measurements have been made of such implementations. The general conclusion is that a mapping over a high-quality OSI Transport Service implementation gives equivalent performance to a mapping over TCP/IP. This is

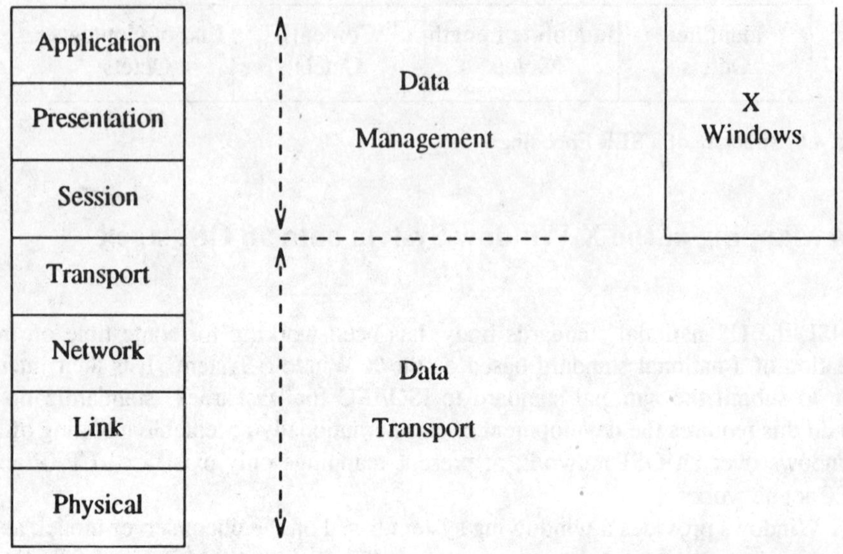

Fig. 4.10. Mapping of X Windows onto an OSI Stack

unsurprising, albeit reassuring. However, mappings over a full OSI stack are found to suffer a performance degradation of one-half to two-thirds of the performance of the TCP/IP equivalent. Some of this degradation can be accounted for by implementation inefficiencies (the measurements have been made largely using prototype versions of the supporting stack), but there has also been found to be a penalty in the mere fact that fully-functional Session and Presentation Services are in use.

These experiments have led to the conclusion within the community that a *lightweight* full-stack implementation is required, supplying *only* those services that X Windows needs. Such an implementation must be efficient whilst retaining conformance to OSI standards, and hence an ability to interwork. The first step is to produce a mapping definition that is carefully constructed to allow a lightweight implementation, but which is aligned to work in progress now within ANSI and later within ISO/IEC so that interworking between implementations is possible.

Such a mapping is being progressed through the auspices of EWOS by various interested parties, mainly although not exclusively in the UK. The project is supplying the effort to edit this document, which has now been completed from the technical point of view and was submitted for ratification in May 1991 as an EWOS 'Technical Guide'. The document will also be issued as a CEN Technical Guide, to ensure wider circulation.

In parallel with the development of the text of the mapping, a trial implementation is being made within the UK academic community. Although not yet complete, preliminary results are encouraging. Under the VMS operating system on a VAXstation, a version of DECwindows mapped to this OSI stack has been found to give a performance penalty on throughput in graphical applications of only 20% compared to DEC's own highly-tuned proprietary network (DECNET). It is expected that further improvements will be possible to the implementation, ensuring virtually identical performance over the two networking technologies. This is extremely encouraging, demonstrating that it is possible to build high-performance OSI applications when careful consideration is given to the design issues involved.

The EWOS mapping will be able to be used as an intercept of any forthcoming ISO/IEC standard. When the latter emerges for 'fast track' it is anticipated that ARGOSI will have a role to play in harmonizing European responses to the draft put forward for standardization. In the meantime work is ongoing in studying a number of areas where X Windows standardization is incomplete. Particular attention is being paid to the subject of the establishment of initial server/client connections in the X Windows environment, an area where there is at present no satisfactory OSI mechanism available.

References

1. – (1987), "Information processing systems – Computer graphics – Computer Graphics Metafile for the storage and transfer of picture description information (CGM), Parts 1–4", ISO/IEC 8632, ISO Central Secretariat.
2. – (1988), "Information processing systems – Open Systems Interconnection – File Transfer, Access and Management, Parts 1–4", ISO/IEC 8571, ISO Central Secretariat.
3. – (1989), "NFS: Network File System Protocol specification", Internet Request for Comment 1094.
4. – (1991), "Improvements to the CGM", in *Graphics and Communications*, ed. D.B. Arnold, R.A. Day, D.A. Duce, C. Fuhrhop, J.R. Gallop, R. Maybury, D.C. Sutcliffe, EurographicSeminars, Springer Verlag.
5. – (1991), "FTAM Constraint Set and Document Type for CGM, Version 1.6", document EWOS/EGFT 91-185, European Workshop for Open Systems.

5 The ARGOSI Demonstrator

5.1 The Demonstrator Scenario

The demonstrator was conceived to illustrate a typical application utilizing graphics and OSI services together and transferring graphical information across international networks. The aims of the demonstrator were:

- to show the feasibility of providing such an application;
- to show how such standard graphics and OSI services could work together;
- to discover what modifications and additions to the standards were necessary to enable these services to work together;
- to provide multiple implementations of the graphics and OSI services to highlight that the interworking of the standards was being demonstrated;
- to demonstrate the prototype application running on distributed heterogeneous hardware networked together;
- to evaluate the success of the demonstrator and to identify what different approaches should be taken in the future.

The choice of prototype application came out of the work on classification (see Chap. 2). An information system for European road freight operators, was identified as the application, and CGM and FTAM (with the CGM document type), as the appropriate standards to provide the required combination of graphics and networking services.

The scenario is that of a road freight operator who wishes to plan a route across Europe, avoiding any traffic difficulties, using a graphical interface. The road freight operator uses the application from a consultation workstation where he is able to draw the proposed route on a map, enter the dates of the journey and request details of the traffic difficulties affecting a journey along this route between the dates. The traffic difficulties falling between the specified dates are displayed on the map together with the route. The map, route and difficulties may be zoomed and panned. The operator may then alter the route or dates to avoid these difficulties and make a further consultation based on the new route.

The aims of the demonstrator (enumerated above) were made specific to the chosen application:

- to show the feasibility of providing the route planning application;
- to show how the FTAM services could be used to transfer the CGM data;
- to discover what modifications and additions to the CGM and FTAM standards were necessary to enable the transfers to take place;
- to provide multiple implementations of the CGM and FTAM software to highlight that the interworking of the standards was being demonstrated;
- to demonstrate the route planning application on heterogeneous hardware located at the partners' establishments linked by the packet-switched public data networks (PSPDNs);
- to evaluate the appropriateness of the use of FTAM and CGM in this application area and to identify to what extent the approach taken can be generalized to other application areas.

This application is typical of a wide class of applications in which a large volume of unchanging data is overlaid with a smaller volume of data which does vary over time and may be held remotely.

5.2 The User's View

This section describes a typical consultation of the system. The initial configuration of the system is shown in Fig. 5.1. Input to the consultation is provided by a mouse and keyboard. Initially the user is presented with a map of Europe, showing major towns and cities, roads, country boundaries and coastal outlines. The commands 'zoom window', 'scale+', 'scale-' and 'pan' enable the user to browse around the map at different levels of detail. The granularity of information displayed depends on the zoom and scale factors. At the highest level of detail (whole of Europe displayed) only major cities and roads are displayed. As the user zooms in on a particular region, more information is displayed, for example minor roads as well as main roads, and names of smaller towns. The command 'whole map' enables the initial view of the map to be restored.

Before a consultation can be performed, the user has to specify the route and the period (specified by a start date and end date) for which hazard information is required.

The menu item 'route points' initiates specification of the route. The route is defined by a sequence of connected lines. A route is input using a multi-button mouse. One button is used to indicate the end of one line segment and the start of a new one. A second button is used to indicate when the route definition has been completed. The line segment currently being defined is echoed to the user as a rubber-band line.

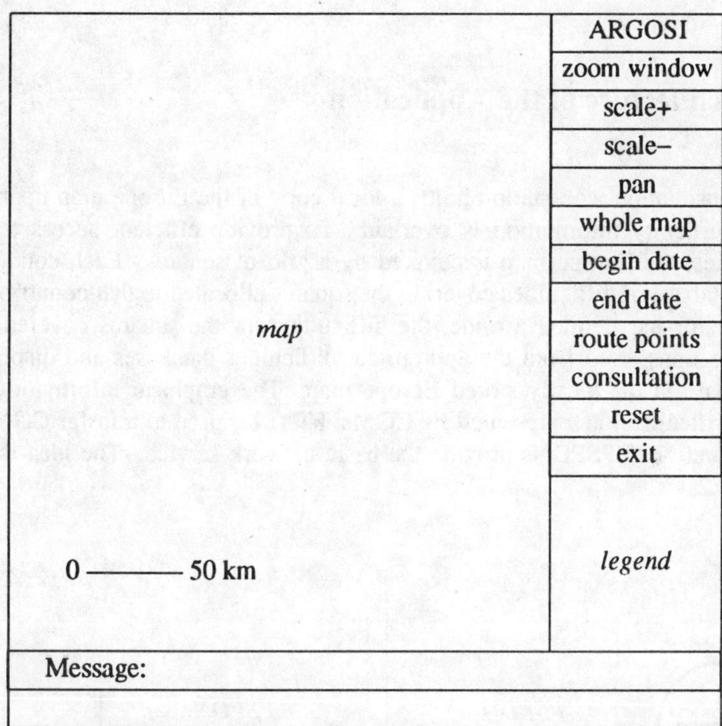

Fig. 5.1. Initial Display Configuration

The begin and end dates for a consultation are entered through the keyboard.

The menu item 'consultation' performs a consultation for the currently defined route between the specified begin and end dates. The results of the consultation are displayed on the map.

Difficulty information is presented to the user in two ways: as patterned areas on the map, or as symbols marking particular points on the map. Patterned areas are used to represent difficulties which may affect a wide area, such as fog, snow and flooding. Symbols are used to represent difficulties which affect a particular location or small area, such as falling stones, road works, slow vehicles and height and weight limits. The meaning of the symbols is displayed in the legend table underneath the menu column.

Once the results of a consultation have been displayed, the zoom, pan and scale commands can be used to focus on a particular region of interest.

The 'reset' command resets the system to its initial state and the 'exit' command exits the system.

5.3 Architecture of the Application

Each consultation workstation holds a local copy of the Europe map upon which traffic difficulty information is overlaid. To provide efficient access to traffic difficulties, the Europe map is covered by a grid of squares. Each country then has a database of difficulties covering the squares allocated to that country. When the operator has defined a route, the difficulties for the squares covered by the route are transferred from the appropriate difficulties databases and displayed as an overlay on the locally stored Europe map. The graphical information (map, traffic difficulties) is represented by CGMs; FTAM is used to transfer CGM information and X.25 PSPDNs provide the basic network service. The idea is shown in Fig. 5.2.

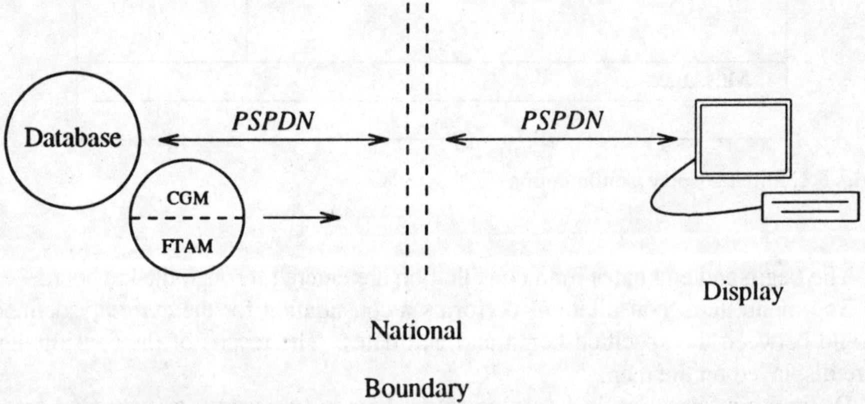

Fig. 5.2. Outline of the Application

At a finer level of detail, the application consists of two independent programs; the consultation program and the creation program. The consultation program is the unit which enables the operator to consult the traffic difficulties. The creation program provides the interface through which traffic difficulties are entered. Both programs were split into application, graphics services and networking services modules for the purpose of design and implementation. The creation program is of less interest than the consultation program and so will not be described further here. The architecture of the consultation program is depicted in Fig. 5.3.

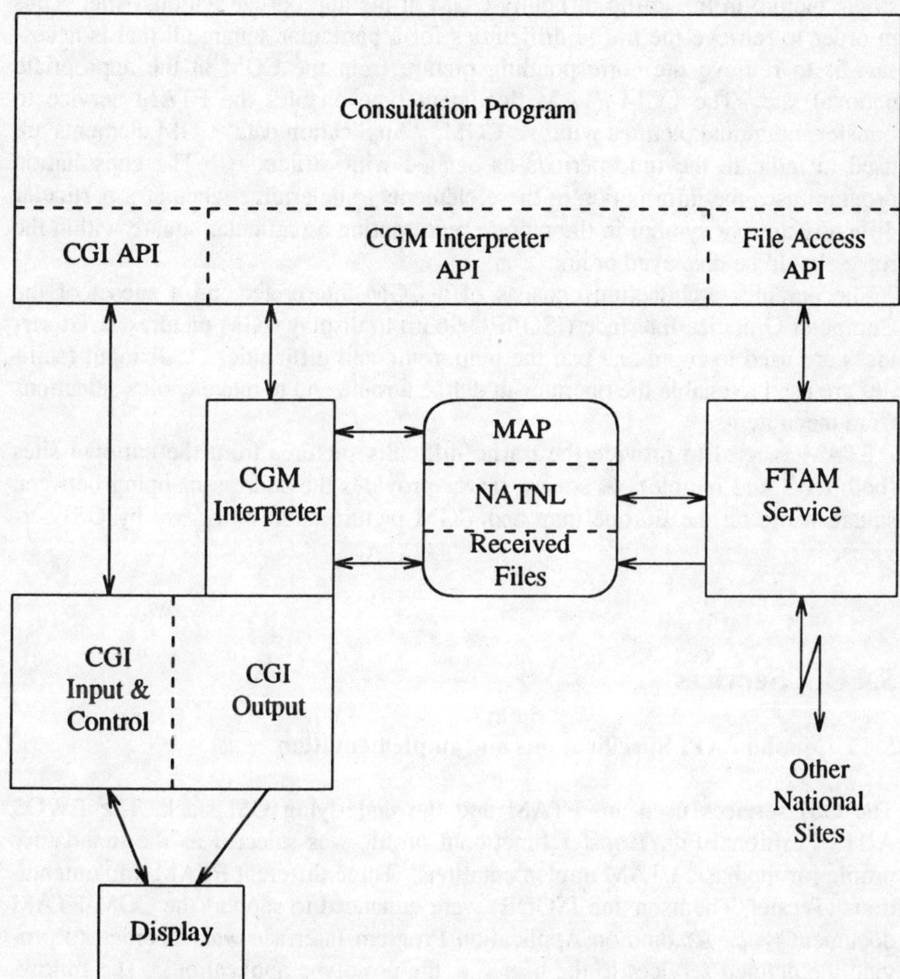

Fig. 5.3. Architecture of the Application Consultation Program

Static information such as road maps is stored at the display point. There is a database of road traffic difficulties associated with each country, which is held at one site (called the national site) in that country. Two types of representation are used for difficulties: symbols at particular positions to represent difficulties such as road works, and patterned areas to represent difficulties which may cover a wide area such as fog and snow.

Each difficulty database is stored as a CGM. The Europe map is logically divided into named squares. All the difficulties within a square are stored within a single picture in the traffic difficulty CGM at the appropriate national site. Thus in order to retrieve the traffic difficulties for a particular square all that is necessary is to retrieve the corresponding picture from the CGM at the appropriate national site. The CGM-FTAM document type enables the FTAM service to transfer individual pictures within a CGM. 'Application data' CGM elements are used to indicate the time periods associated with difficulties. The consultation program uses the information in these elements to determine whether a particular difficulty area or symbol in the picture representing a particular square within the route should be displayed or not.

The graphics architecture consists of a CGM interpreter and a subset of the Computer Graphics Interface (ISO/IEC 9636) to display CGM pictures. CGI services are used to zoom and pan the map, route and difficulties. CGI input facilities are used to enable the operator to define a route and to make choice selections from menu items.

FTAM is used to provide the traffic difficulty pictures from the national sites (both local and remote). A square server provides the address mapping between square name on the Europe map and CGM picture address for use by OSI services.

5.4 OSI Services

5.4.1 Common API Specifications and Implementation

The OSI services used are FTAM and the underlying OSI stack. The EWOS A/112 Positional File Transfer functional profile was selected as the mandatory profile for the basic FTAM implementations. Three different FTAM implementations (Tecsiel, Thomson and ISODE) were enhanced to support the CGM-FTAM document type. A common Application Program Interface was specified to provide the defined services to the user (i.e. the prototype application). The following functionalities had to be provided:

(1) receive a CGM picture from a (possibly remote) filestore;
(2) provide the minimum required set of support functions;
(3) provide asynchronous activation;
(4) allow multiple non-blocking transfer requests;
(5) provide functions to check the status of a transfer in progress.

The result is an API based on the MAP/TOP 3.0 specifications, consisting of the following functions:

(1) fadu_copy – copy a FADU between two filestores;
(2) fadu_wait – get information about a transfer activity previously submitted via fadu_copy;
(3) copy_free – free the space allocated by a fadu_copy function;
(4) ut_address – support function getting all the needed addressing information related to a square.

In the Tecsiel and Thomson case, these functions have been implemented by using the existing interfaces and IPC mechanisms. In the Tecsiel case, for example, the X/FT product already had a high level application program interface. With some adaptations, due to the different data structures involved and to the new capabilities required by the CGM-FTAM document type, the above functions have been implemented on top of existing interfaces. In the ISODE case, it has been necessary to implement the above functions by means of the "System V message queues" Unix IPC mechanism. The application process, at the API level, communicates by "messages" with another process acting as a provider in order to request an FTAM service. There are as many FTAM providers running at once on the local site as remote FTAM responders requested by the application for getting files from remote sites. The FTAM provider is an adaptation of the original ISODE interactive initiator. This solution has proven to be fast enough to implement during the time allocated in the project for this task and quite satisfactory in the context of the prototype application.

The provision of a unique programming interface to the OSI services has proven to be of great help for the specification and implementation of the prototype application, especially because three different FTAM implementations were involved (Tecsiel, Thomson, and ISODE).

5.4.2 First Implementation of a Hierarchical Document Type

A common solution for mapping the FTAM Virtual Filestore to the Real Filestore has been adopted and implemented on the three FTAM implementations.

The following enhancements had to be done in order to implement the CGM-FTAM hierarchical document type:

(1) It was the first introduction of a document type having more than one abstract syntax name in its information objects and this was not handled in ISODE;
(2) The Node-Name type, defined in the ASN.1 module FTAM-FADU, was not fully supported by the FTAM implementations, since Node-Names were not used by previous document types. The implementation of the CGM-FTAM document type required the full support of this type.
(3) The FADU identity SEQUENCE OF NODE-NAMES was not available in any of the three FTAMs, since no previously defined document type could manage this FADU identity.

5.4.3 Three Different Implementations

It is important to emphasize the fact that three different FTAM implementations have been involved, because it is crucial for understanding the development and interworking efforts which have been done. The coordination of the different implementations, the selection of common parts, the verification of interoperability, are some of the problems introduced by the fact of having more FTAM implementations. In order to avoid ambiguities, a Protocol Implementation Conformance Statement (PICS) Proforma was used to specify in a precise way the details of the services to be provided. On the other hand, having three different implementations, running on different hardware (Hewlett-Packard for Tecsiel, CETIA for Thomson, and Sun for ISODE) has demonstrated that the document type definition of a hierarchical document type, as has been done for the CGM-FTAM document type, is possible in a real open environment.

5.4.4 Limitations

The OSI services implemented are a subset of those defined in the CGM-FTAM document type and constraint set definitions. The implemented features represent the minimal subset needed by the prototype application, and have been identified in the PICS. Among the most important limitations, the following should be noted:

(1) Only a subset of the FTAM primitives handling the CGM document type were implemented, mostly F-READ. This corresponds to the functionality required by the prototype application: to access and transfer pictures from a CGM file.

(2) No locate facility: no relative positioning on the elements of the CGM file but always positioning from the root.

(3) The access context used is limited to UA "Unstructured All Data Units" Access Context, as no provision had been made in order to implement easily a different access context such as HA "Hierarchical All Access Data Unit". This development would have required too much effort to justify its inclusion in the project.

(4) No escape sequences are supported.

(5) Supported FADU identities: BEGIN, END, CURRENT, SEQUENCE OF NODE-NAMES.

(6) Only the Transfer service class has been supported.

5.4.5 Performance

The OSI services were implemented and tested. Once the interoperability testing had been performed, the integration of OSI services within the prototype application was effected. Because of lack of available tools, it has not been possible to do a precise performance evaluation, so that the figures obtained are only indicative. However during the Esprit '91 Conference Exhibition there was an intensive week of tests, where the average times to obtain single pictures were found to be in line with the application requirements, where the range 5-15 seconds was identified as the optimum for the application. The time needed to transfer the whole metafile, for example as an unstructured binary file, would have been at least ten times this. In the case of a real application this difference would have been even more noticeable.

5.5 Graphics Services

5.5.1 The Use of Metafiles

The graphics services are composed of a set of modules based on the international graphics standards CGM (ISO 8632 and its Amendments), CGI (ISO 9636) and CGI C binding (ISO 9638).

The CGM tools which have been realized can be subdivided into three parts: generation, editing and interpretation of metafiles. These three basic tools can be used by the same application program at the same time. This requirement had some implications in the design of these tools.

The CGI implementation was primarily realized to serve as a standard interface between CGM interpreters and the display (addressed through the X Window System). It also provided necessary tools for input which were used directly by the application program.

The position of graphics services within the consultation program is depicted in Fig. 5.3. (Note that CGI accesses the display through the X Window System.) The creation program additionally needs to access the CGM generator and editor to modify the difficulty CGMs at the national sites.

The concept of a metafile interpreter has been transformed into the concept of a toolkit composed of the following functions:

INITIALISE INTERPRETATION,
INTERPRET METAFILE DESCRIPTOR,
INTERPRET PICTURE.

INTERPRET PICTURE does not include the operation of clearing the display surface. This operation is left to the application program (i.e. creation or consultation) which decides when it is useful to perform it. The application also has the capability to force reading of elements within a metafile without interpreting them. In the prototype application, APPLICATION DATA elements are used to determine when this operation has to be performed. The application programs do not operate as single interpreters as implicitly defined in the CGM standard. The task which is performed is more complex: composition of pictures and editing of metafiles. This is the reason why some characteristics of a simple interpreter have been modified. The design of these modifications has been done in such a way that it is always possible to reconstruct from the elements, which have been used to compose the picture, a single metafile in a straightforward manner (concatenation of elements).

The composition of pictures is the major difference compared to a "standard" CGM interpreter. The prototype application is built around the idea that the CGM pictures which are managed by it are not independent pictures but can be superimposed to compose the final picture. Two pictures are used as background: the map and the legend pictures and all difficulty pictures are drawn on top of the map. Map and difficulties share the same coordinate system and are drawn using the same VDC extent. Any change to the VDC extent requires redrawing the map and the displayed difficulties in that order. This operation is equivalent to the concatenation of the various elements within the displayed pictures to compose a single picture.

5.5.2 Editing of Metafiles

There was a need, arising from the creation program, for the prototype application to edit metafiles. It was decided to limit these needs to an append capability which allows a picture to be reopened within a metafile and new elements to be added at the end using generator functions. The additional functions needed to implement these facilities are EDIT METAFILE, OPEN PICTURE FOR EDITING and END EDIT METAFILE. A more complete editing capability would have required a data structure to be built, from which elements could be retrieved and modified. This work was not within the scope and the resources of the project. However, the functionality provided could be extended in that direction.

5.5.3 Use of CGM Amendment 1

Another important aspect of this project is the use of the CGM Amendment 1 which was approved by ISO at the beginning of the project. This Amendment adds two major functionalities to CGM which have been extensively used by the prototype application: bundle representations and segments. Bundle representations are used to allow the selection of attribute values to match characteristics of the physical display in a way that does not impact other sites.

The segment capability has been used to represent symbols (road signs). Descriptions of these symbols were stored in metafile descriptors as global segments. Difficulty pictures contain COPY SEGMENT elements to create specific instances of these symbols. This choice was important from a communication point of view since the difficulty pictures are the pictures which are accessed remotely using OSI services. A typical segment contains about 200 octets while the COPY SEGMENT element contains 24 octets. About one hundred occurrencies were used in the demonstration (this number was limited only by the effort put into creating these symbols). This represents a gain of 15200 octets. The use of this facility had an important impact on the feasibility and the success of the demonstration.

5.5.4 Relationship between CGM and CGI

A subset of CGI functions to be used by CGM interpreters was selected. In general, all CGI functions which correspond to a CGM element are included, except for encoding elements which are processed by CGM interpreters and do not influence CGI. However, it was decided not to implement the CGI segment facility for the following reason. Due to the static picture nature of CGM, the full dynamic segment facility of CGI was too powerful and the effort to implement it not justified. For example, CGI provides the ability to delete, rename, pick or reopen individual segments. These functionalities were not required by CGM Amendment 1. This analysis led to the decision to implement segment management within CGM toolkits and not within CGI.

The two CGM toolkits have adopted completely different strategies with respect to CGI use. However, despite these differences, it was impossible to notice which toolkit was used during the demonstration showing the appropriateness of CGI as the interface between graphic devices and CGM interpreters.

5.5.5 CGM Toolkits

The two toolkits used were the LUT-UEA CGM toolkit and the GMD CGM toolkit.

The LUT-UEA CGM toolkit was based on the Loughborough University of Technology's CGM toolkit that was extended, by the University of East Anglia within the project, to incorporate CGM Amendment 1 elements. The basic LUT toolkit was provided free of charge to the ARGOSI project for use in conjunction with the ARGOSI prototype application.

The GMD toolkit was based on an existing toolkit developed by GMD that was extended, by them within the project, to support CGM Amendment 1 elements.

These toolkits consist of collections of library modules that provide procedures for both the generation of CGM elements and their interpretation. They support all three standardized CGM encodings (i.e. binary, character and clear text), but only the binary encoding was needed for the prototype application.

The CGM generator simply provides an encoding method for each of the CGM element types. The extension to the basic generator module of both toolkits to include Amendment 1 elements was straightforwad and did not require additional data types to be encoded.

However, the LUT toolkit ''feature'' that allows for optimization during metafile generation (i.e. by only outputting state setting elements when strictly required) was found to cause some problems when combined with CGM use required by the ARGOSI prototype application. The optimization method also assumes a strict interpretation of the CGM standard with respect to default attribute values in the various initial states of the interpretation process.

Updating of traffic difficulty metafiles, within the prototype application, required basic editing of the metafiles containing the traffic difficulties. This was achieved differently in the two toolkits.

For the LUT-UEA toolkit, an additional interface that provides rudimentary editing facilities, by inserting (or appending) new elements into existing pictures, was also implemented. This ''metafile editor'' module makes use of both the generator and the interpreter parts of the toolkit, but does not use the CGI device driver. In fact, the notional device driver simply regenerates metafile elements in a one-to-one correspondence as existing elements are interpreted. New elements can be inserted into the picture at any stage simply by invoking the desired generator function. The metafile editing facility required by the prototype application limits this functionality to only allow insertion of new elements immediately prior to an END PICTURE element.

In order to provide ''safe'' editing of metafiles, and also due to the capabilities of the operating environment, the ''metafile editor'' makes use of a number of temporary files to copy pictures that are being modified.

For the GMD toolkit, the editing facility was done by copying the metafile in a temporary file up to, but not including the END PICTURE element, adding elements using the generator routines, and finally copying the rest of the original metafile into the temporary file. The original file is then replaced by the temporary metafile. This ''editing'' facility, through rudimentary is sufficient to satisfy the needs of the prototype application.

The CGM standard indicates that a number of different state values are required to be reset to their default settings at the beginning of each picture. The ARGOSI prototype application places collections of traffic difficulties (represented by multiple pictures) on top of a map (also represented by many pictures). Furthermore, these are all drawn inside a window that is managed by a CGI virtual device adjacent to a menu of application commands. In particular, the VDC extent and clip rectangle of the map and menu must be controlled externally to the interpretation of metafiles, particularly since panning and zooming are two of the application functions.

The net effect of this display organization is that the reset to defaults action within the interpreter at each BEGIN PICTURE must be disabled. This limits the use of the thus modified BEGIN PICTURE interpretation function to the specific prototype application.

Outside the ARGOSI context the GMD CGM toolkit (mainly the interpreter) has to work with a large number of output devices. At GMD these devices include devices as different as the X Window System, GKS, CGI, LaserVison displays, QMS-QUIC printers, and PostScript printers. This led to the decision for the

GMD toolkit to handle as much of the additional functionality needed for the ARGOSI project as possible within the interpreter. Because of this the "Aspect Source Flags", bundles and bundle representations as well as the segment processing were handled inside the interpreter and not handed directly to the CGI. This ensured that the software would still be useful after the project.

Another incentive for this decision was the fact that the GMD CGM interpreter had to work with two different CGI implementations (the GESI CGI on Unix machines and the GTS-GRAL CGI on the VMS machine). For example, the GTS-GRAL CGI handles segments, while GESI CGI does not. On the other hand GESI CGI is able to handle bundles and bundle representations, while the GTS-GRAL CGI only allows direct manipulation of attributes.

5.5.6 CGI Implementation

CGI was implemented jointly by GESI and Thomson-CSF within the project. As CGI was less relevant to the integration of graphics and networking within the project, only one project implementation was deemed necessary.

The CGI implementation does not correspond to a specific profile. The initial goal was to implement both CGM and 2-WAY output foundation profiles. However, some restrictions to that goal were introduced. The CGI implementation contains all the functions for the 2-WAY foundation profile except inquiries. All the management of data structures needed for inquiries is performed but the interface was not provided. With a limited amount of effort, it would be possible to extend the library to fulfil this requirement. As to the CGM profile, the following facilities have not been provided: arcs, circles and ellipses, restricted text and append text, management of character sets and fonts. In addition to the requirements of these profiles, all facilities relating to bundle representation were implemented. For input, with the same exceptions regarding inquiries, foundation profiles for stroke, locator and string have been implemented and additional echo and prompt facilities have been provided.

5.5.7 Summary

A number of important issues arose during the development of the graphics services for the ARGOSI prototype application.

The ARGOSI prototype application requires the graphics services to compose a "scene" made up from several "parts," potentially obtained from several pictures, potentially from different metafiles. This requirement is in fact fairly typical of many graphics applications. The CGM standard, while not prohibiting this form of picture composition, includes statements of intent, particularly for the BEGIN PICTURE element, that seem to imply a much simpler concept, e.g. it states that the display surface should be cleared and certain attributes and control values should be reset to their default values upon interpretation of the BEGIN PICTURE element. In the prototype application, these actions needed to be avoided, and both toolkit implementations achieved this by modifying the interpretation of this element. In general, this solution is not appropriate since it has the effect of affecting picture independence. However, a clean solution to this problem is not obvious since a special action to be taken on interpreting this element will require detailed modification of the toolkit.

The LUT-UEA toolkit generator originally incorporated an optimization feature that minimized the number of attribute setting elements in the metafiles it generated. The optimization would only output attribute setting elements when required for the correct rendition of graphic primitive elements and only when the attribute values were different from the current state. The optimization therefore assumed a strictly sequential and contiguous order to the interpretation of a picture within a metafile. With the prototype application's use of APPLICATION DATA elements to control subsequent element interpretation, this assumption was no longer correct, resulting in incorrect attribute settings in some cases during interpretation. The conclusion here is that if the circumstances in which metafiles are interpreted is unknown or known to be non-sequential, then control over optimization should be provided.

Ideally, the CGM interpreter (including the device driver portion) could assume sole use of a freely available set of devices/graphics resources, such as attribute values, colour table entries, etc. Similarly the application using the CGI virtual device could also make this assumption. In practice, some conflicts can arise when the application effectively overloads the use of certain attribute and control values that the interpreter is also using, e.g. by changing an attribute value behind the interpreter's back. This is a case of the general problem of resource sharing between competing entities but, with care, problems can be avoided.

The decision to use CGI to provide graphical input and output, was taken at a stage when it was believed the prototype application would do all its graphical output through the interpretation of CGMs. CGI, as discussed earlier, is eminently suitable for this task. However, subsequently it was realized that the prototype application would need to perform graphical output directly (particularly in the creation unit). It was also realized that, on account of the decision not to use CGI segments, redrawing operations required re-interpretation of CGM pictures. In retrospect, it might have been better to use a higher level standard graphics system, such as GKS, to provide the graphical input and output. This would have given access to higher level graphical facilities, like support for transformations and segment storage, that would have improved the architecture of the prototype application.

5.6 GDF to CGM Format Converter

The prototype application required the use of a map of Europe in CGM format. Obtaining access to such a map was not easy. Finally it was decided to obtain a map of Europe in Geographic Data File (GDF) format from Michelin and to produce a format converter from GDF to CGM within the project.

The GDF standard has been defined to specify the exchange format of the geographic data. A GDF file consists of records, each record containing several fields which are record type dependent. The line, the polygon, and the spot record types have a feature_code field which gives the geographical feature of the record. The format converter program converts GDF polygons to CGM polygons for countries, islands and urban areas. It converts GDF lines to CGM polylines for borders, motorways and roads. The GDF name record type is converted to CGM text for city names.

The GDF attribute_values record type has been used by the format converter to produce three detail levels of the Europe map, for use within the prototype application according to the display zoom factor. The lowest detailed level (3000 km for the square side) contains one picture, the medium level (1600 km) 15 pictures and the highest detailed level (600 km) 41 pictures. Each picture is stored in a CGM metafile. For each level, an initial filter is applied to the GDF coordinates to remove all redundant points according to a four by four pixels resolution on the screen.

5.7 How did the Prototype Application Meet the Aims?

5.7.1 Introduction

As outlined in Sect. 5.1, the prototype application was conceived as a typical application to illustrate the integration of standard graphics and OSI Services achieved within the ARGOSI Project. The chosen application required the use of graphics and networking services. The prototype application was designed to be able to use such services based on international standards. As anticipated at the start of the project, the then current standards were insufficient on their own to enable this to be achieved. The project defined a CGM document type for FTAM (and had it accepted for inclusion with the international standard list) and made use of standards under development to complete the objective.

5.7.2 Meeting the Aims

In Sect. 5.1, the aims of the ARGOSI demonstrator are listed in relation to the route planning application. In this section, each of those specific aims will be considered as to how far they were met.

Feasibility. One of the initial tasks of the classification work was to select an appropriate application for use as a prototype. Arising from interviews with various organizations developing applications which use graphics and networking, one set of applications stood out as being suitable for study. These were inherently spatial and distributed.

In these applications, which are drawn from application areas such as transport planning and meteorology, there is a useful distinction between high volume but slowly changing data (for example, the background map) and the dynamic data (for example, weather patterns). In some situations this dynamic data is low volume and useful savings can be made by only transmitting this data.

In several application areas, it was commonly found that a user was consulting a portion of existing graphical data.

These features led the project to consider a prototype application based on consultation of graphical data in a geographical application area. The fact that this led to the successful production of the prototype application demonstrates the feasibility of producing such an application.

Use of FTAM to transfer the CGM data. CGM is an international standard file format for the storage and transfer of graphical information. It was designed to be transferred, *inter alia,* across networks. FTAM is an international standard for the transfer of files across OSI networks. As such, FTAM can be used to transfer whole CGMs across networks. FTAM was used in this manner to transfer the Europe map CGMs to the various sites prior to running the application. CGM proved to be a satisfactory tool to store the Europe map.

However, the requirement of the prototype application was more demanding than this in that parts of CGMs needed to be transferred. FTAM provides the means to do this through the concept of a document type, which allows the structure of a file to be specified to FTAM. By defining a CGM document type for FTAM (as described in Sect. 4.2) and providing support for this document type within the FTAM implementations, the requirements of the prototype application were met: metafile descriptors, pictures within metafiles, and complete metafiles were able to be transferred.

Modifications and Additions to CGM and FTAM. The prototype application required the transfer of pictures within CGM files and the composition of several pictures in displaying the results.

As described in the previous section, the former was achieved via the specification of a new document type for FTAM. This CGM-FTAM document type was specified within the project and progressed through the appropriate standardization process for inclusion with the international standard list.

The CGM-FTAM document type described a CGM file as a three-level hierarchy. This allowed access to complete metafiles and individual pictures within a metafile. A further level could have been added to provide greater functionality, i.e. access to segments within pictures. However, segments within CGM Version 2 (CGM incorporating Amendment 1) are context sensitive and, without restrictions on how the CGMs were generated, could not be accessed individually. Consideration should be given to removing the context sensitivity from segments in CGMs. From the document type point of view, the resulting document type would have been significantly more complex.

The composition of several pictures is described in Sect. 5.5.1. In order to achieve this in the manner described, it was necessary to use a common metafile descriptor for the legend metafile and traffic difficulty metafiles at all the sites. This is perfectly acceptable and just a matter of agreement between the sites. Conversely, the relaxation of the requirements on interpreting BEGIN PICTURE, so that different pictures can be superimposed, contravenes the standard and consideration should be given to rewording the CGM standard in this area so that more flexible CGM interpretation can take place.

The selective interpretation of the traffic difficulty metafiles, based on the data in the APPLICATION DATA elements, placed requirements on the use of optimization in generating these metafiles. The conclusion was that the application using the generator should have control over what optimization takes place. This is a requirement on the generation software rather than the CGM standard.

Interworking of Standards. Much care was taken within the prototype application workpackage to define the interfaces between the application and the graphics and OSI services and between the components of the services. As previously described, many of the interfaces were based on the standards in use or the APIs to those standards. This enabled several implementations of the standards used to be employed in different realizations of the prototype application. The common APIs to the two sets of services have been documented.

Three implementations of FTAM (Tecsiel, Marben (from Thomson), and ISODE) were used, each extended to provide support for the CGM-FTAM document type. Two different CGM toolkits, both extended to provide support for Version 2 CGMs, were used for the generation and interpretation of CGM metafiles, using a common CGI for graphical input and output. Each of the common applications (consultation and creation) made use of the different FTAM and CGM software in different combinations. The FTAM implementations interworked exchanging CGM data and the CGM toolkits were able to interpret CGMs produced by each other. The whole prototype application highlighted the interworking of graphics and OSI standards together and with each other.

Demonstration of Route Planning Application. The route planning application was demonstrated on the ARGOSI stand at the Esprit '91 Conference Exhibition. The consultation program was demonstrated on a Sun SPARCstation 2, a CETIA workstation and a Hewlett-Packard workstation at the exhibition. These workstations were connected to the Belgian PTT's public X.25 network. National sites were provided by a Sun server at RAL, UK (for the UK), the CETIA workstation at the exhibition (for France), a Sun workstation at INRIA, France (for Germany), a Hewlett-Packard workstation at Tecsiel, Italy (for Italy and central Europe), and a Sun workstation at COSI, Italy (for southern Yugoslavia and Greece), connected to the respective national X.25 networks. All three FTAM responders were used to give access to the traffic difficulty CGMs. The consultation program was used with both the CGM interpreters and all three FTAM initiators.

The application was successfully demonstrated throughout the duration of the exhibition. Routes were planned across the whole of Europe and traffic difficulties fetched from each of the national sites. Visitors to the stand were impresssed by the demonstration.

Evaluation. This aim was to evaluate the appropriateness of the use of FTAM and CGM in this application area and to identify to what extent the approach taken can be generalized to other application areas.

The route planning application was demonstrated successfully in the manner envisaged when the application was conceived. As has been reported earlier, the transfer times were in line with expectations and sufficient for the requirements of the prototype application. The display times were similarly satisfactory so that the whole prototype application could be used as a real-time demonstration.

The use of CGM to store the traffic difficulties and the use of FTAM with the CGM-FTAM document type worked well and showed how standards could be used in a realistic application.

Several observations have already been made about the individual services. A further observation concerns the interworking of the graphics and OSI services. The CGM standard made careful provision for pictures within a metafile to be accessed individually and non-sequentially. However, because it did not specify the storage format but merely the contents and encoding, the mechanism for accessing individual pictures was not specified.

In the prototype application, the FTAM responder needed to access individual pictures within the metafile to return to the consultation program and the CGM interpreter needed to access individual pictures within the map metafile (although this latter was subsequently altered.) For the FTAM requirement, an indexing function was added to the FTAM responder to record, in an index, the location of the individual pictures within the CGM. This function was invoked the first time a file was accessed by FTAM but the index was retained for further use.

The basic LUT CGM interpreter read a CGM file sequentially to find individual pictures, which was time consuming for large metafiles such as the initial Europe map CGMs. A UEA enhancement was to use the indexing function, written for FTAM, to generate an index, so improving the performance of searching for a picture significantly. Thus, the two different services used by the prototype application were performing the same operation.

This leads to a more general point about the implementation of the CGM-FTAM document type. While its specification and implementation were successful, the strategy needs to be considered further in the light of the possible appearance of many more FTAM document types in the future. In the ARGOSI implementation, knowledge of the document type, and the files it described, was built into the FTAM responder. However, the document type only related to one of the three possible encodings for CGM and only represented a CGM with a three-level hierarchy (as discussed earlier). To have included support for those extra features would have needed considerably more software to be added to the responder. Thus, it may not be feasible to provide built-in support for all document types when a large number come into existence. Secondly it resulted in the FTAM service needing to do a partial implementation of the CGM interpreter to generate the index, which needed to be done elsewhere by the CGM tools. Consideration needs to be given to how document types can be implemented without building all the knowledge into the FTAM service.

5.7.3 Summary

In summary, the route planning application has been found to meet the aims of the workpackage in the following ways:

- the successful design, implementation, and demonstration of the route planning application demonstrated the feasibility of producing such distributed applications;
- FTAM was successfully used to transfer complete CGMs between sites and CGM proved to be a satisfactory tool to store the Europe map;
- the definition of the CGM-FTAM document type (and the provision of its support within the FTAM implementations) enabled metafile descriptors, pictures within metafiles, and complete metafiles to be transferred but consideration should be given to changing the CGM standard to remove the context sensitivity from segments in CGMs and to allow more flexible CGM interpretation to take place;
- three European implementations of the FTAM international standard and two European implementations of the CGM international standard interworked to transfer graphical information across international networks;
- the route planning application was successfully demonstrated running on heterogeneous hardware (CETIA, Sun and Hewlett-Packard) located at the partners' establishments;
- the use of FTAM and CGM in conjunction served the prototype application well but consideration needs to be given to how document types can be implemented without building all the knowledge into the FTAM service.

5.8 Conclusions

The selected prototype application, a route planning application, was successfully designed, implemented, and demonstrated running on heterogeneous hardware (CETIA, Sun and Hewlett-Packard). Three European implementations of the FTAM international standard and two European implementations of the CGM international standard interworked to transfer graphical information across international networks. The CGM-FTAM document type was produced and a number of important observations and suggestions for change in the current standards were made. This will lead to an improvement of standards in this area.

6 The ARGOSI Workshops

6.1 Graphics and Communications

This EUROGRAPHICS international workshop on Graphics and Networking took place from 15-17 October, 1990, organized by the ARGOSI project. As part of the research it was proposed that a number of workshops would be run, bringing together experts from the graphics and networking areas, in order to examine relevant issues about the interactions of the two. This was the first such workshop which was held in Breuberg, Germany. The workshop was attended by 29 invited participants from 8 countries.

6.1.1 Structure

The workshop was run in eight sessions over the three day period with papers presented in the first six sessions followed by a session of parallel small group discussion of some of the questions resulting from the presentations. The workshop concluded with a plenary session to which the small groups reported their discussions. The results of this discussion are summarized in Sect. 6.1.4.

The first session was an introduction to the workshop, the ARGOSI project and the overlap between graphics and networks.

The second session focussed on the current uses of networking and graphics and included presentations on the ODA standard for interchanging compound documents, a distributed application involving use of two 64Kbit/sec channels and a description of the work on classification of graphics applications undertaken in the ARGOSI project.

Four sessions of papers were presented on the second day. The two sessions in the morning concentrated on access to large volumes of remotely stored graphics with six presentations covering a number of topics. In the first session the standards requirements for MIS systems for road transport management, the BERKOM broadband interconnect trial and the PIC metafile format were presented. The second session looked at the various aspects of the CGM standard's applicability in networked applications with presentations describing CGM's relation to

FTAM and to the concept of application profiles, and the use of access to subunits within CGMs.

A number of presentations on the afternoon of the second day focussed on the theme of distributed interactive graphics. The afternoon began with a paper describing current standards efforts in Image Interchange. Four of the papers which followed over the two sessions looked at aspects of the relationship between ISO/IEC work in graphics and networking and the X system. There were also extra papers presented on the STEP product interchange standard, and practical issues in using CGMs in a heterogeneous environment.

The sessions of presentations concluded with one describing some of the new problems to be faced in implementing networked multi-media applications.

A paper by C.T. Little on the requirements placed on graphics and networking by applications in meteorology was also input to the discussions although the author was unfortunately unable to be present at the workshop.

6.1.2 Discussions

Following the final presentation the group spent some time analyzing themes which appeared to have recurred in the discussions following each paper. Six major topics were identified.

Impact of multi-media

A range of related issues arose from considering future directions which multi-media applications, including voice and video as well as generative graphics, would require. Given the difficulties encountered in merging the use of current networks and graphics there was a strong feeling that further extension to other media would be complex and that in addition there would be new problems in synchronization of the various streams of information. Synchronization would require new network services and there was concern over the migration of such applications into OSI environments.

Relationship of X to standards

Given the number of papers in which various aspects of the relationship between X and its various components and ISO standards were considered, it was clear that this was an area of concern to participants. Of particular concern was that, given the fixed functionality of the X protocol and the consequent need to use the extension mechanism to accommodate additional functionality in support of graphics standards (e.g. PEX), the end result could easily be a large number of extensions (e.g. one or more for each standard) and consequently enlarged server with less guarantee of any particular X server providing the full range of extensions. Another important concern was that a system with fixed functionality would become obsolete in the foreseeable future. If this was a real expectation would it be worth the efforts needed to define and improve the interworking of X and other standards? Given the effort required perhaps the area would be best ignored in the expectation that a new, readily extensible, protocol would be defined in the medium term, rather better integrated with other ISO efforts.

Improvements to the CGM

A group of topics for discussion were identified as potentially requiring revisions to improve the CGM standard. These topics covered such things as requirements for network access to metafiles including random access to individual pictures or even segments. This implied the need to limit the context sensitivity of the CGM which is defined as an ordered (and hence context sensitive) sequence of elements. There were also a number of issues related to encoding of metafiles which had arisen in the presentations. Finally the use of a heterogeneous environment incorporating different implementations of CGM generators and interpreters has consequences for the range of implementation latitudes that can be allowed while still generating a successfully networked application.

The role of profiles

In many areas of standardization the concept of application profiles was being used to refine the definition in a standard by tying down areas of implementation latitude, specifying minimum and maximum requirements etc. It was clear to participants at the workshop that such profiles were being used for a variety of purposes including:

- improving the definition of ''faulty'' standards;
- satisfying the requirements of interoperability for particular application areas;
- defining escapes and other entities.

In view of this variety of purposes the workshop decided that some further investigation to define appropriate use of the profiles concept was necessary. Other concerns in the area related to the International Standardized Profile mechanism in ISO/IEC JTC1, which was reported as allowing a profile relating to any standard to become officially recognized by ISO/IEC without reference to the committee which originated the standard.

Image Interchange standards

Although only one paper had been presented specifically on this topic, the influence of possible standards in this area on the implementation of multimedia and other networked applications was clear. The workshop therefore felt that topics such as the definition of Image Interchange Format objects and the mechanisms by which they could be moved across OSI networks merited further discussion. There was also debate about whether this was an area to which the ARGOSI project should make a specific contribution.

ARGOSI classification taxonomy

A number of application areas which had been described had suggested possible alternative metrics or refinements to metrics within the ARGOSI Classification scheme for graphics applications networking requirements and other characteristics.

6.1.3 Discussion Groups

The workshop then split into three groups examining the topics of multi-media, improvements to the CGM, and the role of application profiles. Whilst the other topics were also felt to be important there was insufficient time for further work in these areas and they remained topics for future efforts.

6.1.4 Summary and Conclusions

The Workshop concluded with a final session. Following the presentation of the Working Group reports, the three sets of recommendations were integrated and, where appropriate, augmented to generate a set of recommendations for the workshop. In view of the links between the Role of Profiles Working Group and the Improvements to CGM Working Group, these were considered first, beginning with the former.

It was agreed that profiles were finding increasingly wide application and concern was expressed that even amongst current proposals it was clear that they were being used in inappropriate ways. The following actions were recommended.

- Define a framework and a set of ground rules for profiles for use with standards.
- Review current proposals for profiles in the light of this work.
- Study whether profiles can be expressed through proformae.
- Gain a familiarization with the International Standardized Profile (ISP) mechanism (pursuing any changes that might arise) and explore its use for profiles for standards for graphics and networking.

The working group examining improvements to the CGM then presented their results and as a result the following actions were recommended:

- Submit a CGM defect report recommending a change of name of the 'character' encoding to be 'octet' encoding and to clarify the standard to avoid future confusion. This should prevent some of the potential conflicts which arise if the Character Encoding is interpreted as expressing meaning through the character as opposed to the bit pattern of the octet as listed in the standard. The proposed FTAM document type was flawed as a result of misunderstanding in this area and should be corrected.
- Produce an ASN.1 encoding for the CGM and explore the most appropriate way of standardizing this. Consider whether a partial ASN.1 encoding to express the CGM structure and using an existing encoding for the content would be useful.
- Produce a CGM profile to constrain the use and ordering of certain CGM elements to allow independent access to segments within CGMs conforming to the profile.

- Study what elements should appear in metafile and picture descriptors in a CGM.

The actions arising from the Multi-Media issues Working Group were discussed with the result that the following actions were recommended:

- Study the use of connection-oriented protocols in multi-media.
- Explore the use of lightweight protocols in multi-media.
- Study the needs and architecture of multi-media applications and explore the abstractions necessary to include computer graphics in multi-media. (Note that there is a need for a multi-media paradigm for new applications, a sort of multi-media reference model.)

The Workshop was considered a success by all the participants and there was a common desire to disseminate the results of the Workshop to others interested in the area of graphics and communications. The proceedings were published by Springer-Verlag (D.B. Arnold *et al.*, *Graphics and Communications*, EurographicSeminars series).[1] A list of the papers included in the proceedings is given below.

- R.A. Day, D.A. Duce, J.R. Gallop, R. Maybury and D.C. Sutcliffe, *P2463: The ARGOSI Project for ISO/IEC Graphics and Networking Standards.*
- G.S. Carson, *Graphics, Networking and Distributed Computing.*
- P.J. Robinson, *Office Document Architecture (ODA). The Standard for Compound Document Interchange.*
- D.E. Lewis, *Multipoint Protocol Aspects of Audiovisual Teleconferencing via one or two 64Kbit/s Channels.*
- J.R. Gallop, *The ARGOSI Classification Scheme for Graphics and Networking Applications.*
- C.T. Little, *Meteorological Communications and Graphics.*
- P. Egloff, *Multimedia Applications in a Broadband Environment. Framework for Integrated Services.*
- J.F. Mortelmans, *Towards Standards for Combining Database, Knowledge Base and Communication Technologies in the Field of Road Transport Management.*
- W.D. Fellner and F. Kappe, *PIC – A Metafile Format for Distributed Graphics Applications.*
- P. Artico, F. Dilonardo and M. Re, *An Overview of the FTAM Standard and its Applications to CGM File Transfer.*
- A.M. Mumford, *Application Profiles and the CGM.*
- A. Ducrot, *Access to Segments in a Version 2 CGM Metafile.*
- J. Dyer, *X Windows over OSI.*
- G.J. Reynolds and D.B. Arnold, *CGI Profiles for Use with X.*
- D.B. Arnold, S. Th. Liapakis, G.J. Reynolds and N.P. Vezirgiannis, *Transporting CGMs Between Implementations. Some Practical Considerations.*

- S.J. Noll and M.G. Schendel, *The Graphics Standards PHIGS and GKS-3D in an X Window System Environment.*
- G.R. Hofmann and C. Blum, *The Image Model and the Image Interchange Format.*
- R.E. Brennan, *Integration of X Applications with Open System Standards: Panacea or Pariah?*

6.2 Distributed Window Systems

The first ARGOSI Workshop recognized the importance of distributed window systems and the position of the X Window System in the market place. There was insufficient time to address the issues of distributed window systems in the discussion groups and so a separate workshop on Distributed Window Systems was organized.

The theme of the Workshop was the appropriateness and role of distributed window systems for distributed graphics applications. Contributions were sought exploring these ideas. Areas of interest listed included:

- experience with X and other window systems for distributed graphics applications;
- reference models for distributed graphics applications and windowing;
- impact of high bandwidth communications on requirements for high performance distributed graphics applications.

The Workshop was held at The Cosener's House, Abingdon, UK on 9–11 December 1991 and was attended by 29 participants from 6 countries.

6.2.1 Structure

The Workshop was run in eight sessions over the three day period with papers presented in the first six sessions, followed by a session of parallel small working group discussions of issues arising from the presentations. The Workshop concluded with a plenary session to which the working groups reported their discussions. The conclusions of the plenary session are included in Sect. 6.2.3, along with recommendations for further work arising from these conclusions.

The first session opened with an introduction to the Workshop and the ARGOSI project. The remainder of the first session and the second session focused on architectural issues. The emerging ISO/IEC Reference Model for Computer Graphics was described in the first paper along with an outline of the ARGOSI classification scheme and the relationship to window systems.

Subsequent papers discussed the problems of X in the context of remote working, interactive access to distributed graphics, the ARGOSI demonstrator, the role of window systems and distributed computing in scientific visualization, and topics in the use of distributed window systems in interactive telematics services.

The third session contained an informal presentation on work in progress at the University of Michigan on video networks and a demonstration of the ARGOSI demonstrator.

The second day contained three paper sessions. The first addressed issues in distributed processing: ISO/IEC work in terminal management standardization, the evolution from OSI (Open Systems Interconnection) to ODP (Open Distributed Processing) and distributed user interface systems. The remaining two sessions looked at some current distributed window systems and associated problems. The current status of the PEX activity was described, followed by a paper on the XGL object-based graphics library for the X environment. Work to extend X to allow "window sharing" between multiple workstations, motivated by requirements of a tutoring environment, was presented. The final paper session contained a discussion of some of the problems with designing user interfaces for remote working, with particular reference to X, followed by a description of the approach being taken at Santa Clara University to solving the latency problems inherent in current LAN protocols for graphics intensive applications.

6.2.2 Working Groups

Following the paper presentations, the Workshop spent time elucidating and organizing the issues that had been raised by the papers and the discussions after each. It was decided to split into three discussion groups under the broad headings:

- future directions for X;
- other distributed window systems;
- models for processing in distributed window systems.

Each working group was assigned a list of issues to start the discussion. On the final day, the Workshop reconvened in plenary session to hear reports from each of the working groups. These formed the basis for the formulation of the conclusions and recommendations of the Workshop.

6.2.3 Conclusions and Recommendations

The final session of the Workshop was a plenary discussion based on the working group reports. Many of the topics discussed arose from discussion in more than one of the working groups. Therefore they were grouped in terms of the topics rather than in relation to the working groups where they were originally discussed. Consequently discussion was divided into two main parts:

- X as a specific window system;
- distributed window system models at large.

The method adopted was to assert at the beginning of this plenary session a number of conclusions, based on the reports of the Working Groups. These were then debated, and modified as necessary as a result of the discussion, and a set of recommendations were subsequently produced. The final recommendations are given in the ensuing sections of this chapter as highlighted paragraphs, each numbered bold in square brackets – e.g. **[10]**.

It was evident throughout the Workshop that the influence of X permeated every discussion, irrespective of whether the topic specifically concerned this particular window system. This is perhaps not surprising and merely demonstrates that X is the only *distributed* window system for which there is at present a substantial body of practical experience.

X as a Specific Window System.

Extensions to X: There was discussion about potential extensions to X conflicting with each other or introducing concepts that are inappropriate to a distributed window system. However it proved difficult to formulate a precise statement on these points without losing desirable capabilities.

There are a number of different scenarios regarding the use of extensions. For example, the video extension for X (VEX) introduces new facilities that are not possible with unextended X (in this case video input); the PHIGS extension for X (PEX) allows the client to delegate some graphics processing to the server but does not introduce new windowing facilities. The extension providing support for non-rectangular windows adds functionality to the server, but this does add to the windowing facilities available. Hence it is necessary to distinguish between the introduction of new functionality, that does not reasonably fit into the model of X functionality (which is presumably that of a window system), and the introduction of functionality that can sensibly be regarded as that of a window system. The criterion for deciding this might be whether or not a new resource type is being introduced but this of course depends upon a clear understanding of what resources may be considered to be controlled by unextended X! Where the functionality added departs from that which could reasonably be expected of a window system alone, it may be better to consider the resulting client and server as implementations of (for example) VEX and not of X.

There was strong concern expressed that unbridled use of extensions will lead to mass incompatibilities between the capabilities of clients and servers. In principle the extension mechanism is fail-safe in that it incorporates a bilateral negotiation between client and server as to the acceptability of each extension that the client wishes to use. In practice this will only be the case if the client's behaviour when a negotiation fails is as helpful as possible. For example, a site may make a big investment in X servers today, and be unable to run future X clients. This could come about because such an X client might require the use of an X extension even where, in principle, a plausible mode of operation without the extension exists.

Such lack of adaptability already exists in many X clients which (unnecessarily) assume the use of a particular X visual class for colour.

Two recommendations are made in this area.

[1] *A Registration Authority and mechanism should be created for X extensions. Part of the registration procedure must include the provision of a statement of the fallback strategy expected of a client when a server cannot support an extension.*

This will aid in the writing of conformance statements for both clients and servers, the urgent need for which was noted by the Workshop. Such mechanisms exist for ISO/IEC standards in computer graphics and (more recently) for OSI and it may be possible to handle registration of extensions using such an existing mechanism if and when X undergoes ISO/IEC standardization. In the meantime, there is an urgent need for an interim arrangement (e.g. a mechanism set up by an ISO member body, such as ANSI, who could support their national standardization of X in this way).

The second recommendation concerns the nature of extensions themselves.

[2] *There should be further study to define a model for X extensions and, in particular, to define under which circumstances an extension of X is a valid method of achieving the desired functionality.*

X Input Facilities: The working group on future directions for X identified a mismatch between input and output facilities. One example is PEX, where the definition group (for historical reasons) did not define input facilities to match the extended output facilities. The result is that the client needs to provide the resources to handle input that could otherwise be delegated to the PEX server. Also the input modes of PHIGS are not adequately supported.

Further problems were identified, in cases where a user's actions provide input that requires a very quick response but incurs a lengthy round trip across a long-haul (or other high latency) network.

These observations lead to the following recommendation.

[3] *There should be further study of the graphics input facilities provided by X. This should aim towards the definition of an input model in which the semantic richness in levels of output distribution already available in X can be matched by corresponding richness in levels of input distribution.*

Protocol Optimization in X: The bandwidth of a network connection limits the flow of data across that connection. For high rates of data transmission across low bandwidth networks, some compression is needed. There are a number of situations where knowledge of the content may introduce improved compression ratios compared with what the networking services can achieve without that knowledge. Even where there is such knowledge available to the networking services, it is not clear that this would be of practical use. In OSI terms, this would be handled by the Presentation Service, by the recognition of a suitable transfer syntax that incorporated an appropriate compression scheme for the transfer of data and corresponding decompression upon receipt. This would imply that compression is handled by the Presentation Service component of an implementation. Normally, however, this would be a general-purpose product, implementing at most one or two of the OSI standard transfer syntaxes (such as the Basic Encoding Rules).[3] Thus it may be obligatory in practice that the application itself, with its own specialized knowledge of what would be an appropriate compression scheme, performs this function.

One common situation is for the transfer of images, where (for some user defined level of acceptable loss of quality) the JPEG[4] and MPEG[2] methods can allow full colour images to be transmitted with less than a bit per pixel and still be recognisable. In contrast, another situation is for the transfer of geometric graphics information, where JPEG and MPEG are not appropriate to the compression of large sequences of points. Other compression methods, possibly application-specific, might be needed in such cases.

These observations lead to the following recommendation.

[4] *Standardized compression schemes for graphics data should be included in the X Data Stream Definition for transfer of the corresponding data types.*

It was noted that bandwidth is not the only restriction on performance. Latency in a network affects the time delay between a request leaving the user's terminal or workstation and the response returning to the user. Long-haul networks typically possess high latency (often because of speed-of-light considerations, as well as those of the number of "hops" through intermediate switches on the journey), but the latter consideration applies to some short-haul networks as well. Various solutions were suggested, such as inserting the high-latency step at a place which ensures that the functions local to the X toolkit remain close to the user (e.g. on the user's local network). However such solutions must avoid hard-wiring toolkit functionality into the server, as this may militate against the client's policy on look and feel.

Other ways to improve interactive performance over high-latency networks can be identified, based usually on the adoption of a synchronous-mode terminal protocol or a similar model. However, these usually result in loss of functionality as users attempt to run applications originally developed for use over high-performance networks over lower-performance networks.

These observations lead to the following recommendation.

[5] *Effort should be directed towards the development of better and more appropriate ways to distribute applications, rather than simple reliance on a window system to effect the distribution. This will require a better understanding of the requirements relating to distribution, specific to an individual application, rather than the assumption that there is a single, generic solution.*

Security in X: The ability for clients to share bitmap information is an advantage in many situations, such as co-operative working. However for applications requiring security, despite recent improvements (particularly with respect to the use of X's own authentication mechanism, support for which is included as part of the Data Stream Definition), it is still too easy for clients to eavesdrop on each other. This seems to be primarily a matter of user education – it was felt that, whilst the current authentication mechanism within X is by no means perfect, the problem is that its existence is not widely appreciated. Although there is a danger of informing potential eavesdroppers of this fact, there is an even greater danger of users that require security not being aware of the loopholes.

This observation leads to the following recommendation.

[6] *The present status of security in X should be made more widely known. This should be done by vendors ensuring that users of their implementations are able to make use of the existing authentication mechanism by ensuring that their documentation brings this to the users' notice.*

The topics both of eavesdropping, and of access control and authentication, are general distributed system issues and solutions developed in the general case need to be adopted by X. The aim should be for it to be possible both to make a server secure against unauthorized clients and to make one client secure against others with respect to both input and output (i.e. client-to-client security), via the use of suitable authentication and access control, possibly supplemented by data encryption techniques in cases where this is necessary. (It should be noted that data encryption may not be needed to prevent the type of client-to-server eavesdropping of common concern at the present – this is accomplished by a client persuading a server to supply information, e.g. a bit map, and hence should be preventable by appropriate access control. Data encryption should necessary only to prevent physical eavesdropping, e.g. on an Ethernet.)

Time and Service Definitions in X: There are a number of obvious examples of the use of graphics over a window system where the concept of time is important. Animation requires the delivery of a sequence of pictures at precisely controlled intervals. Multi-media requires the synchronization of multiple streams of data. Both are examples where time is important in X. A less obvious example arises with the PEX implementation, where it was found (after implementation) that, with a single-threaded server, a long-running PHIGS operation executing in the server (such as a traversal) effectively "freezes" the window system for all other operations (e.g. a window resizing) during that time. The net result is a poor response to the user from the window system.

It needs to be recognized that such problems are not exclusively to do with X and hence cannot be solved without more general solutions. However, there are some aspects specific to X – e.g. the PEX issue given above.

The need to specify time constraints on operations implies a need for a *service definition* for X, in which the treatment of time would be an essential component. Such a service definition would also be helpful in the treatment of X extensions, in that it should make it easier to understand how the functionality added by the extension relates to the basic service provided by X. There is also evidence, gained from the experience of developing a mapping of X onto an OSI network, that the current lack of a clear description of the X service makes treatment of X as part of a distributed system considerably harder. (In this case it led to problems in understanding what the Abstract Syntax for X was, and consequently how to separate this from its Transfer Syntax in order to make a clean mapping onto the Presentation Services provided by OSI.)

The "Quality of Service" concept in the ARGOSI Classification Scheme may provide relevant input to such a service definition.

Initially it might be thought that there is also a link with the OSI Quality of Service concept as well. However, OSI treats Quality of Service as a Session Layer concern, although the application informs the Session Layer of its requirements in this respect. Thus the X application itself would still need to have an understanding of the Quality of Service being demanded of it, in terms of its own operations, and then to translate those aspects pertaining to the underlying communications into suitable requests on the Session Service.

These observations lead to the following recommendation.

[7] *A service definition should be developed for X. This should treat the issue of time dependence in certain of the services offered and should also take into account the need to operate in an OSI environment.*

Conclusions on Distributed Window System Models at Large. This section applies to distributed window systems other than X and also to more general distributed application models.

Distributed Applications: Discussion in the Models working group, followed by the plenary discussion on network latency in X, highlighted the need to consider performance in the more general context of distributed applications. It was seen that, although the issues are wider than simply the need to cope with variable-latency networks, this specific issue merely highlights a weakness in the design of X itself.

As noted already, the distributed window system is an easy place to put the "cut line" when designing a distributed application. It was also noted that, in the case of X, it is not necessarily the best and, in some situations, is a quite poor position to make the cut. This may be due to the limitations of X, but it may also be that, in some cases, no distributed window system, however rich in functionality, offers the correct solution. It is necessary first to decide how best to distribute applications, then to choose services to do this best.

The Relationship between Windowing and CGRM: The Workshop was not able, in the time available, really to come to grips with the general topic of the relationship between a window system and the CGRM. Part of the problem was that the non-existence of a satisfactory model for the window system provided by X (the only exemplar available for which there is a body of experience!) made substantive progress virtually impossible.

The only conclusion drawn was that in developing the relationship between a distributed window system and the CGRM, one should look at a programming interface (such as Xlib and similar services, in the case of X). The important point is that an understanding is needed of the functionality that is transported and not necessarily of the mechanism by which this is done.

Distributed Window System in Terminal Management: The work on Terminal Management within ISO/IEC is aimed towards a general mechanism for the treatment of interactive systems (e.g. terminals, graphics workstations, multimedia systems), designed to fit the OSI model. As such it is to be welcomed as of value in assisting in the development of models for distributed window systems.

Assuming that the current standardization work gets sufficient impetus to drive it forward, Terminal Management may provide a basis for second-generation window management systems. To assist in this work, and to ensure that sufficient generality is built into the standards, there is a need for expert contributions to the Terminal Management work, from those active both in window system design and more generally in graphics.

The Workshop felt that the name "Terminal" Management deceives people active in the field of window systems into thinking that this work has nothing to do with workstations. The phrase "Presentation Resource" Management was suggested, but not seriously considered unless it is possible to agree what is meant by "Presentation". It also conflicts with the existing use of the term Presentation in OSI. However, a more descriptive word than Terminal is needed in the name Terminal Management.

These observations lead to the following recommendation.

[8] *The ISO/IEC standardization work on Terminal Management should be promoted more actively to those involved both in distributed window system design and in the use of graphics in such an environment. They in turn should be encouraged to contribute their expertise to this work.*

Resource Management: The resources managed by distributed window systems are only part of the overall picture of resource management in distributed systems. There is a need for more work on models of resource management, for example to encompass the requirements of Computer Supported Co-operative Working, which include sharing of window resources between multiple users or applications. The distributed window system's resource management facilities then need to be harmonized within the general model.

Summary of Recommendations. The following is a summary of the recommendations of the Workshop.

[1] A Registration Authority and mechanism should be created for X extensions.

[2] A model for X extensions should be developed, to include a definition of the limits of applicability of this technique.

[3] A model for graphical input within X should be developed, to match the semantics of existing graphical output facilities.

[4] Standardized compression schemes for graphics data should be included in X.

[5] A more general model for the distribution of graphical applications should be developed, to overcome the need to rely solely on a window system (such as X) to achieve distribution.

[6] Existing facilities in X for security should be made more widely known to the user community, via appropriate action by vendors.

[7] A service definition should be developed for X, to include the concept of time dependence and to recognize the need to operate in an OSI environment.

[8] The ISO/IEC work on Terminal Management should be promoted more actively, with a view to involving experts in the areas of window systems and of graphics.

6.2.4 Proceedings

The proceedings of the Workshop were published by the European Association for Computer Graphics, P.O. Box 16, 1288 Aire-la-Ville, Switzerland, as *Distributed Window Systems Theory and Practice,* D.B. Arnold, R.A. Day, D.A. Duce, J.R. Gallop and D.C. Sutcliffe (Eds), Eurographics Technical Report Series, EG 91 AR, ISSN 1017-4656. A list of the papers appearing in the proceedings is given below.

- D.A. Duce, *The Computer Graphics Reference Model.*
- C. Cartledge, *Remotely Through an X Window.*
- G. Faconti, F. Paternó and C. Giuliano, *An Interactive Approach to Distributed Graphics Systems.*
- A. Ducrot, C. Hieaux, M. Planes, R.A. Day, D.A. Duce and D.C. Sutcliffe, *The ARGOSI Application Demonstrator.*
- J.R. Gallop, *Scientific Visualization on Distributed Window Systems.*
- S. Vrind, *Distributed Window Systems in Telematic Services.*
- J. Dyer, *ISO/IEC Terminal Management Standard and Related Work.*
- G. Schürmann, *The Evolution from Open Systems Interconnection (OSI) to Open Distributed Processing (ODP).*
- S. Freeman, *Deconstructing the Workstation.*

- S.W. Thomas, *PEX: Status, Directions and Alternatives?*
- R. Hagy and P. Maillot, *XGL: A Case Study of the Design of a Graphics Interface.*
- M. Altenhofen, B. Neidecker-Lutz and P. Tallet, *Upgrading a Window System for Tutoring Functions.*
- N.M. Maclaren, *Approaches to Some Wide-Area Windowing Problems.*
- N.M. Maclaren, *User Interfaces and Remote Working.*
- H.S. AlKhatib, *A Light-weight Protocol for LANs to Support Graphic-Intensive Applications.*
- S.W. Thomas, *Using Video Networking for Distributed Graphics.*

References

1. D.B. Arnold, R.A. Day, D.A. Duce, C. Fuhrhop, J.R. Gallop, R. Maybury, and D.C. Sutcliffe (Eds) (1991), *Graphics and Communications,* EurographicSeminars series, Springer-Verlag.
2. D. Le Gall (April 1991), "A Video Compression Standard for Multimedia Applications", *CACM* **34**(4), pp.47–58.
3. International Organization for Standardization (1987), "Specification of Basic Encoding Rules for Abstract Syntax Notation One (ASN.1)", ISO 8825.
4. G.K. Wallace (April 1991), "The JPEG Still Picture Compression Standard", *CACM* **34**(4), pp.31–44.

- [illegible] PEX [illegible]
- [illegible]
- [illegible]
- [illegible]
- [illegible]
- [illegible]
- [illegible]

References

1. [illegible] Arnold, [illegible] A. Day, D. Andrews, C. [illegible], R. [illegible], R. [illegible] and D. Sanchis (Eds.) (1991), [illegible], Springer-Verlag.

7 Evaluation of the Project

7.1 Demonstration at the 1991 ESPRIT Exhibition in Brussels

The first public demonstration of the ARGOSI application was given at the 1991 ESPRIT Exhibition, which was held in parallel with the 1991 ESPRIT Conference. The exhibition took place at the Palais des Congres in Brussels. For five days, starting on the 25th and ending on the 29th of November, 125 ESPRIT projects exhibited their major results. The exhibition featured projects from six areas:

Microelectronics
Information Processing Systems and Software
Advanced Business and Home Systems – Peripherals
Computer-Integrated Manufacturing and Engineering
Basic Research
Information Exchange Systems

The ARGOSI project was presented as one of the 'Advanced Business and Home Systems – Peripherals' projects, and the subarea 'Open Access to Information'.

To demonstrate the interworking of hardware and software from different vendors due to the use of international standards three machines were brought to Brussels for the exhibition. All three machines were from different manufacturers (CETIA, Sun, and Hewlett-Packard) and each of them demonstrated a different combination of OSI and graphics software. The CETIA Unigraph used Marben FTAM and the CGM software from GMD, the Sun SPARC used ISODE FTAM and LUT-CGM software, while the Hewlett-Packard 6000 used Tecsiel FTAM and GMD-CGM software. All three machines were connected to national traffic difficulty servers in the UK, France, Italy and Greece over an X.25 link.

The availability of three workstations at the exhibition had two additional advantages. More than one demonstration could be given at the same time. Since the exhibition was connected to the conference, Conference attendees tended to visit the exhibition during the conference pauses, leading to a large number of visitors during these periods, which made the ability to perform two or three demonstration in parallel a useful asset. The second advantage came from the fact that we would have been able to get the demonstrator running locally (with national databases distributed over the three machines in Brussels) in case there were problems with the external X.25 link. Fortunately this wasn't necessary, but it included a useful safety margin in case something went wrong.

Visitors were usually given a ten minute demonstration of the system together with information about the use of standards in graphics and networking. During the demonstration phase a route was drawn on the Europe map (to avoid the impression of a 'canned demo' the visitor was often asked to propose a route) and a time period was entered. After the consultation, when the traffic difficulties along the route were shown, the pan and zoom functions were used to show areas of special interest. Following that the travel dates were changed to demonstrate how graphic information could selected from the CGMs based on different requests from the application. After the demonstration visitors had the chance to ask further questions or to get some 'hands on' experience with the system.

The most often asked question was 'Is the information data really coming over the network at this moment or are they all stored locally?' Due to a data buffering mechanism in the software, information once received was never transferred again, so in a lot of cases the data *was* stored locally. Fortunately it took just a simple restart of the application to clear the local buffer files and force the application to actually request the data from the remote sites. Visitors were usually impressed by the fact that the results still arrived reasonably fast (typically within less than one minute, depending on the congestion on the network), given the fact that often three or four servers had to be queried.

The presentation of the ARGOSI project was generally well received and managed to get on the list of about a dozen projects which were recommended presentations for VIPs to visit.

7.2 Dissemination of Results

The following section contains information about how the results of the ARGOSI project have been disseminated to international standardization bodies and via contributions to workshops and conferences. In addition the dissemination of the ARGOSI achievements can be seen by the presentation of the ARGOSI demonstrator in various places.

7.2.1 Input to Standardization Bodies

The members of the ARGOSI consortium have mainly worked in working groups of the International Organization for Standardization (ISO) and in the European Workshop for Open Systems (EWOS). In ISO the main effort was expended in activities of SC21 – especially to the FTAM group – and in activities of SC24 – especially the development of the Computer Graphics Interface (CGI) and the further development of the Computer Graphics Metafile. The main direction of the ARGOSI contribution to EWOS can be seen in the registration of the FTAM document type for structured CGM.

A good European harmonization of the standardization activities in the graphics area has been reached through the chairmanship of the SC24 Working Group 3 where two people from the ARGOSI consortium have been in charge: D.B. Arnold (UEA) and A. Ducrot (INRIA) respectively.

7.2.2 Registration of CGM-FTAM Document Type

The successful registration of the CGM-FTAM Document Type was mainly driven by the ARGOSI partners TECSIEL (Pisa – I) and COSI (Milan – I). Both have prepared several technical contributions for and participated themselves in standardization meetings of SC21/WG5 and the EWOS Expert Group on File Transfer (EGFT). As a result an internationally agreed document is available describing the CGM-FTAM document type and constraint set.

7.2.3 Finalization and Publication of ISO/IEC 9636 (CGI)

The dissemination of the ARGOSI project in particular can be seen in directly converting knowledge into the standardization process of the Computer Graphics Interface CGI. The fact that the final editing process of the International Standard CGI was done by the ARGOSI partner UEA (Norwich – GB) guaranteed the direct information flow of ARGOSI results into the standardization discussions. ISO/IEC 9636 (parts 1-6) was finally published in December 1991.

7.2.4 Finalization and Publication of Amendments to ISO/IEC 8632 (CGM)

During the last 3 years the ARGOSI project had a strong influence on the technical progress of the development, the finalization and the publication of Amendment 1 and Amendment 3 of the International Standard 8632 – Computer Graphics Metafile. Errors and technical problems were identified during the implementation process of the ARGOSI demonstrator and forwarded to the particular technical committee. Additional functionality was proposed for inclusion in the amendments. Several members of the ARGOSI consortium (INRIA – F, GMD – D) have contributed to the further development of the CGM. During the life time of the ARGOSI project two amendments of CGM were published.

7.2.5 Transfer Formats for CGM Based on ASN.1

Three ARGOSI partners (RAL – GB, COSI – I, GMD – D) have been engaged in the development of an ASN.1 description of ISO/IEC 8632 – CGM, and the construction of a prototype tool for generating ASN.1 encodings of CGM metafiles according to the ASN.1 Basic Encoding Rules. The interim results have been forwarded to the technical committee of ISO/IEC where these contributions have been appreciated. It has been stated that in the near future a more detailed discussion of the technical problems should be undertaken.

7.3 Contribution to Workshops and Conferences

Under the umbrella of the ARGOSI project two major workshops (see Chap. 6) have taken place where actual results of the ARGOSI project have been presented and discussed with experts from the specific areas.

The first international workshop on Graphics and Networking was held in Breuberg in Germany from 15 to 17 October, 1990. The motivation for the workshop was in line with the general approach of the ARGOSI project: to bring the development of international standards of the networking and the computer graphics area together. In total 19 position papers were presented to 29 invited participants from 8 countries. The position papers as well as the results of detailed discussions and the conclusions have been published in the EurographicSeminars series (Springer Verlag).

The overall results of the first ARGOSI workshop mentioned above were presented by several members of the ARGOSI consortium at the joint SIGGRAPH/SIGCOMM workshop which took place on January 16-18, 1991 in Boulder / Colorado (USA). It was noted in this workshop that the ARGOSI taxonomy for graphics and networking applications represents a good framework for classifying new visualization applications. Continued collaboration between the two communities – in Europe and in USA – was recommended.

The second international ARGOSI workshop dealt with Distributed Window Systems – Theory and Practice. It took place at The Cosener's House, Abingdon in the United Kingdom, from 9-11 December 1991. 29 participants from 6 countries discussed the presented position papers under the view of theory and practice. The position papers together with the results and conclusions have been published as a Eurographics Technical Report.

Additionally ARGOSI results were presented and disseminated in conferences taking place all over Europe (e.g. Graphics in ESPRIT in conjunction with the Eurographics Conferences in Montreux and Vienna, contribution to ESPRIT technical week in Brussels).

7.4 Summary of Achievements

The achievements of the project compared to the four aims stated in the Technical Annex to the Consortium's Contract with the CEC (quoted in section 1.1) are considered in this section.

(1) *The development of software tools and packages to assist in the construction of applications which use graphical transfer over wide-area networks.*
The most important contributions under this heading are:
- three FTAM implementations have been upgraded in order to provide the functionalities needed by the FTAM-CGM document type.
- two CGM implementations have been enhanced to handle the additional elements for segments defined in CGM Amendment 1.
- an implementation of CGI functionality over X Windows to display CGMs.

(2) *An improvement of both the quality and applicability of Standards in the area of graphics and of the application of OSI standards to the transfer of graphical objects.*
The ARGOSI project has produced the CGM FTAM document type and this into the standardization process, and has demonstrated the practical utility and applicability of this approach to building distributed graphics systems. The contribution made by ARGOSI to the development of the EWOS Technical Guide on X over OSI mapping. Although the CGM ASN.1 work is incomplete, the project has taken a significant step in trying to harmonize graphics and OSI standards in this important area. Problems have been identified and a genuine opportunity for collaborative work between ISO/IEC working groups in OSI and Computer Graphics and Imaging has been created. The contribution of the project to strengthening cooperation between European nations in Computer Graphics and Imaging standardization ought not to be dismissed too hastily.

(3) *The development of a detailed understanding of how to construct systems which use Graphics and OSI networking. This understanding will be applicable across a wide range of applications domains.*
This is the most difficult objective against which to quantify the achievement, but although achievement here is somewhat intangible, it is in many ways the most important objective of the project. Partners who are in the business of building real distributed systems for real customers, have had the opportunity to evaluate in detail one particular approach (access to subunits of graphical information through FTAM) in the context of a realistic prototype application. This experience will undoubtedly influence and indeed is already influencing, the approach taken to building distributed systems in these organizations. There is now at least one peg in the design space, where real experience has been gained. The classification work also provides a contribution to a design methodolgoy (synthesis and analysis) for systems which use graphics and OSI networking. It would be a gross exaggeration to claim

that this is in anyway a complete methodology, but it does draw attention to a number of key factors which a system designer would be well-advised to keep in mind whilst working.

(4) *An investigation into the validity of currently available wide-area networking facilities via a practical demonstration involving a prototype within a suitable application domain.*

The demonstration has showed that it is possible to use existing wide area public networks to access bulk graphics data, in terms of the availability and reliability of the networks involved. It has also shown that, by careful management of the amounts of data transferred, it is possible to achieve useful results even at very low bandwidths. The techniques used to obtain this degree of management depend on both the properties of the OSI services involved (e.g. the use of the access capabilities of FTAM) and of the graphics services involved (e.g. the use of segments within the CGM to encapsulate commonly-used picture elements which needs to be transferred only once). Although at the outset of the ARGOSI project it was generally believed that the advent of higher bandwidth services would mean that less care would be needed in the economical use of bandwidth. However, three years later, it is still the case that even in Western Europe the bandwidths generally available on public networks are essentially those used in the project. It seems unlikely that there will be significant penetration of higher bandwidth services at economic tariffs for some time. In addition, the recent changes in Eastern Europe make it clear both that public networks there will be developed over the next decade, and that these will necessarily be of low bandwidth for the foreseeable future. Thus it remains important to continue to cater for this sector of network services.

Appendix 1 – Summaries of Throughput Results

The following diagrams summarize the mean throughputs seen into and out of each site.

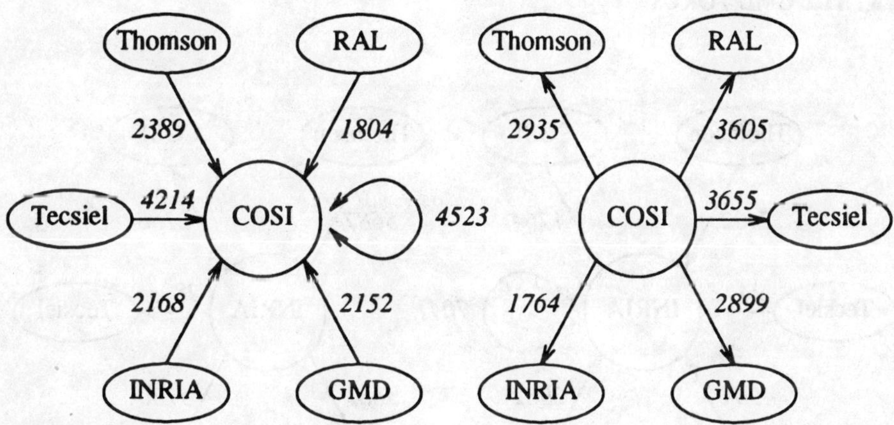

Fig. A1.1. COSI

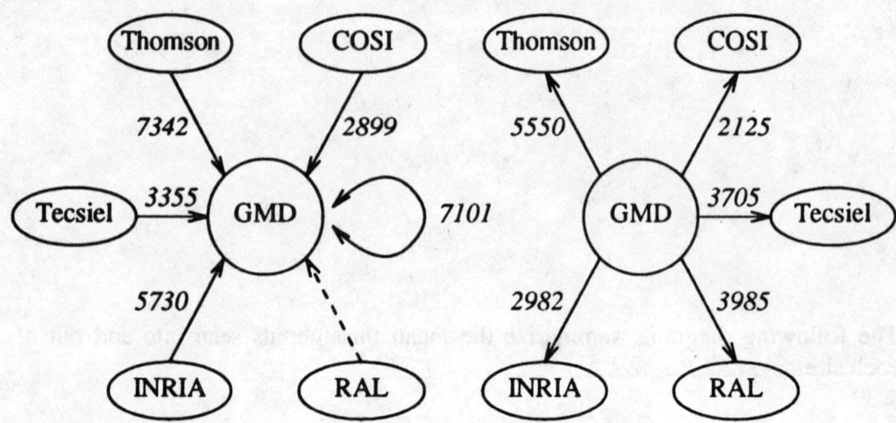

Fig. A1.2. GMD-FOKUS

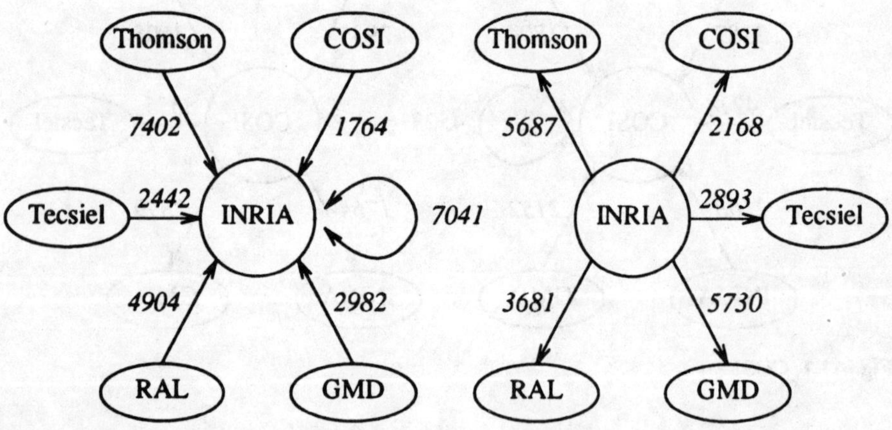

Fig. A1.3. INRIA

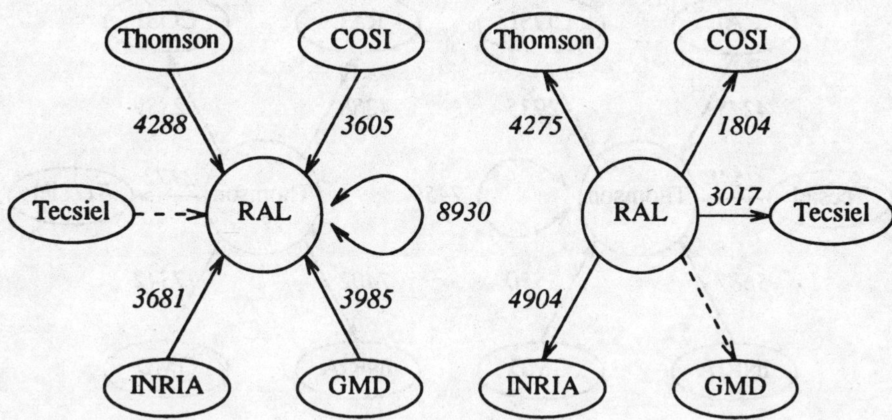

Fig. A1.4. RAL

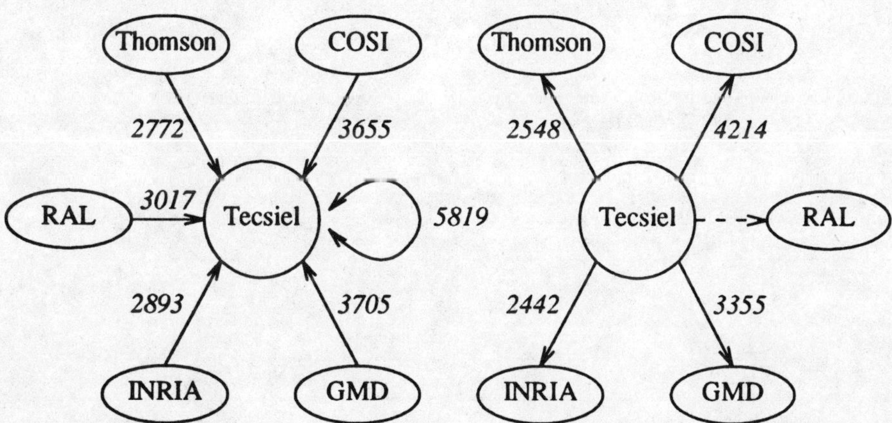

Fig. A1.5. Tecsiel

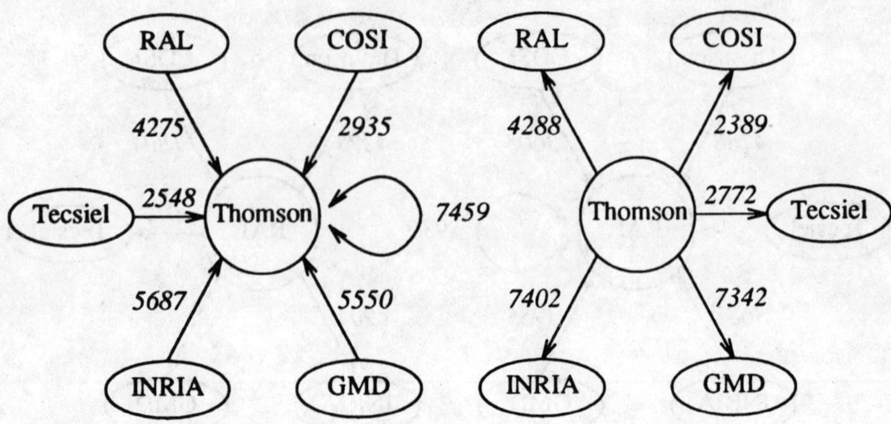

Fig. A1.6. Thomson CSF

Appendix 2 – Call Failures

The following table gives the calling and called sites for the call failures described in Table 3.14.

Table A2.1. Call Failures Analysed on Calling/Called Site Basis

Calling site	*Called site*	*Number of calls failed*	*Reason for Call Failure* loc. host failure	network congestion	network other	unknown reason
COSI	INRIA	4				4
	Thomson	3				3
GMD	COSI	1	1			
	INRIA	2		2		
	Thomson	1		1		
RAL	INRIA	6	2	1	3	
Tecsiel	GMD	3	2	1		
	INRIA	5		3	2	
	RAL	1		1		
	Thomson	2		2		
Thomson	COSI	1	1			
	Tecsiel	1				1
	INRIA	1				1
	RAL	4				4

Appendix 3 – ASN.1 Notation for CGM Subset

The following is the notation in ASN.1 of a subset of the CGM that was used to develop the prototype tools for encoding of a CGM into BER, and subsequent decoding.

```
-- Representation of an ISO 8632 Version 1 CGM

CGM-version-1 { iso standard 8632
                version-1-abstract-syntax(1) }
DEFINITIONS IMPLICIT TAGS ::=
BEGIN

CGMetafile ::= SEQUENCE {
   beginMetafile [0] IA5String DEFAULT "",
                   -- metafile identifier parameter
                 [1] MetafileDescriptor,
                 [2] SEQUENCE OF Picture
                     OPTIONAL,
   endMetafile   [3] NULL }
                     -- ie no parameter to element

MetafileDescriptor ::= SEQUENCE {
   metafileVersion      [0] INTEGER (1),
                     -- metafile version number parameter
   metafileDescription  [1] IA5String,
   elementList          [2] MetafileElementList,
   optionalDescElmnt    [3] SEQUENCE OF DescElmnt OPTIONAL
                                     }

Picture ::= SEQUENCE {
   beginPicture       [0] IA5String DEFAULT "",
                     -- picture identifier parameter
                      [1] SEQUENCE OF
                          PictureDescriptorElement OPTIONAL,
```

```
    beginPictureBody [2] NULL,
                     [3] SEQUENCE OF
                         PictureBodyElement OPTIONAL,
    endPicture       [4] NULL }
                      -- ie no parameter to element

 PictureDescriptorElement ::= CHOICE {
    scalingMode                     [0] SEQUENCE {
     mode                                [0] ENUMERATED {
                                              abstract(0),
                                              metric(1) },
     metricSclFctr                       [1] REAL },
    colourSelectionMode             [1] ENUMERATED {
                                         indexed(0),
                                         direct(1) },
    lineWidthSpecificationMode      [2] ENUMERATED {
                                         absolute(0),
                                         scaled(1) },
    markerSizeSpecificationMode     [3] ENUMERATED {
                                         absolute(0),
                                         scaled(1) },
    edgeWidthSpecificationMode      [3] ENUMERATED {
                                         absolute(0),
                                         scaled(1) },
    vDCExtent                       [5] VDCRectangle,
    backgroundColour                [6] RGB }

 PictureBodyElement ::= CHOICE {
                                    [0] ControlElement,
                                    [1] GraphicalElement,
                                    [2] AttributeElement }

 MetafileElementList ::= SEQUENCE OF ElementName

 ElementName ::= ENUMERATED {
              -- all GCM elements currently defined
                 drawingSet(0),
                 drawingPlusControlSet(1),
                 beginMetafile(2),
                 endMetafile(3),
                 beginPicture(4),
                 beginPictureBody(5),
                 endPicture(6),
                 metafileVersion(7),
                 metafileDescription(8),
                 metafileElementList(9),
                 vDCType(10),
                 maximumColourIndex(11),
                 colourValueExtent(12),
```

```
                    metafileDefaultsReplacement(13),
                    scalingMode(14),
                    colourSelectionMode(15),
                    lineWidthSpecificationMode(16),
                    markerSizeSpecificationMode(17),
                    edgeWidthSpecifictionMode(18),
                    vDCExtent(19),
                    backgroundColour(20),
                    auxiliaryColour(21),
                    transparency(22),
                    clipRectangle(23),
                    clipIndicator(24),
                    polyline(25),
                    disjointPolyline(26),
                    polymarker(27),
                    polygon(28),
                    polygonSet(29),
                    cellArray(30),
                    rectangle(31),
                    circle(32),
                    circularArc3Point(33),
                    circularArc3PointClose(34),
                    circularArcCentre(35),
                    circularArcCentreClose(36),
                    ellipse(37),
                    ellipticalArc(38),
                    ellipticalArcClose(39),
                    lineBundleIndex(40),
                    lineType(41),
                    lineWidth(42),
                    lineColour(43),
                    markerBundleIndex(44),
                    markerType(45),
                    markerSize(46),
                    markerColour(47),
                    fillBundleIndex(48),
                    interiorStyle(49),
                    fillColour(50),
                    hatchIndex(51),
                    patternIndex(52),
                    edgeBundleIndex(53),
                    edgeType(54),
                    edgeWidth(55),
                    edgeColour(56),
                    edgeVisibility(57),
                    fillReferencePoint(58),
                    patternTable(59),
                    patternSize(60),
                    colourTable(61),
```

```
                    aspectSourceFlags(62) }

DescElmnt ::= CHOICE {
    vDCType   [0] ENUMERATED {
                  integerVDCType(0),
                  realVDCType(1) },
    maximumColourIndex
              [1] INTEGER,
    colourValueExtent
              [2] SEQUENCE {
                  minColourValue      [0] RGB,
                  maxColourValue      [1] RGB },
    metafileDefaultsReplacement
              [3] SEQUENCE OF
                  CHOICE {
                   controlElement
                     [0] ControlElement,
                   pictureDescriptorElement
                     [1] PictureDescriptorElement,
                   attributeElement
                     [2] AttributeElement }
                     }

ControlElement ::= CHOICE {
    auxiliaryColour     [0] Colour,
    transparency        [1] ENUMERATED {
                            off(0),
                            on(1) },
    clipRectangle       [2] VDCRectangle,
    clipIndicator       [3] ENUMERATED {
                            off(0),
                            on(1) }
                        }

GraphicalElement ::= CHOICE {
    polyline              [0] PointList,
                      -- note requires at least two points
    disjointPolyline      [1] PointList,
                        -- note requires even number of points
    polymarker            [2] PointList,
                        -- note requires at least one point
    polygon               [3] PointList,
                        -- note requires at least 3 points
    polygonSet            [4] PointEdgePairList,
                        -- note requires at least 3 points
    rectangle             [5] PointList,
                        -- note must be of size 2 points
    circle                [6] Circle,
```

```
    circularAr              [7] PointList,
                        -- note requires 3 points
    circularArc3PointClose
                            [8] SEQUENCE {
                                [0] PointList,
                                 -- must be length 3
                                 closeType     [1] CloseType },
    circularArcCentre       [9] CircularArcCentre,
    circularArcCentreClose
                            [10] SEQUENCE {
                                 [0] CircularArcCentre,
                                 [1] CloseType },
    ellipse                 [11] PointList,
                              -- must be length 3
    ellipticalArc           [12] EllipticalArc,
    ellipticalArcClose      [13] SEQUENCE {
                                 [0] EllipticalArc,
                                 [1] CloseType },
    cellArray               [14] CellArray}

Circle ::= CHOICE {
    integerCircle    [0] SEQUENCE { -- for integer VDCtype
                         centre     [0] IntegerPoint,
                         radius     [1] INTEGER (0..MAX) },
    realCircle       [1] SEQUENCE { -- for real VDCtype
                         centre     [0] RealPoint,
                         radius     [1] REAL (0..MAX) }
    }

CircularArcCentre ::= CHOICE {
    integerCircularArcCentre
                     [0] SEQUENCE {
                         [0] IntegerPoint,
                         [1] SEQUENCE SIZE (4) OF INTEGER,
                         [2] INTEGER (0..MAX) },
    realCircularArcCentre
                     [1] SEQUENCE {
                         [0] RealPoint,
                         [1] SEQUENCE SIZE (4) OF REAL,
                         [2] REAL (0..MAX) }
    }

EllipticalArc ::= CHOICE {
    integerEllipticalArc
                     [0] SEQUENCE {
                         [0] SEQUENCE SIZE (3) OF
                              IntegerPoint,
                         [1] SEQUENCE SIZE (4) OF INTEGER },
```

```
    realEllipticalArc
                        [1] SEQUENCE {
                             [0] SEQUENCE SIZE (3) OF RealPoint,
                             [1] SEQUENCE SIZE (4) OF REAL }
     }

CloseType ::= ENUMERATED {
    pie(0),
    chord(1) }

CellArray ::=  CHOICE {
    integerCellArray
                        [0] SEQUENCE { -- for integer VDCtype
                             [0] SEQUENCE SIZE (3) OF
                                   IntegerPoint,
                             [1] SEQUENCE SIZE (2) OF INTEGER,
                         -- note LocalColourPrecision omitted
                             [3] ColourArray },

    realCellArray  [1] SEQUENCE { -- for integer VDCtype
                             [0] SEQUENCE SIZE (3) OF RealPoint,
                             [1] SEQUENCE SIZE (2) OF INTEGER,
                         -- note LocalColourPrecision omitted
                             [3] ColourArray }
                             }

ColourArray ::= CHOICE {
    indexedColourArray [0] SEQUENCE OF INTEGER,
    directColourArray  [1] SEQUENCE OF RGB
                             }

AttributeElement ::= CHOICE {
                             [0] LineAttribute,
                             [1] MarkerAttribute,
                             [2] FillAreaAttribute,
                             [3] ColourTable,
                             [4] AspectSourceFlags }

LineAttribute ::= CHOICE {
    lineBundleIndex      [0] INTEGER (1..MAX),
    lineType             [1] DefinedLineType,
    lineWidth            [2] CHOICE {
                                  [0] CHOICE {
                                    -- absolute linewidth
                                       [0] INTEGER,
                                         -- for integer VDCtype
                                       [1] REAL },
                                         -- for real VDCtype
                                  [1] REAL },
```

```
                                     -- scaled linewidth
    lineColour           [3] Colour }

DefinedLineType ::= INTEGER {
        -- note 0 not allowed
        solid(1),
        dash(2),
        dot(3),
        dash-dot(4),
        dash-dot-dot(5)
        }

MarkerAttribute ::= CHOICE {
    markerBundleIndex     [0] INTEGER(1..MAX),
    markerType            [1] DefinedMarkerType,
    markerSize            [2] CHOICE {
                              [0] CHOICE {
                               -- absolute marker size
                                  [0] INTEGER,
                                   -- for integer VDCtype
                                  [1] REAL }
                               ,   -- for real VDCtype
                              [1] REAL },
                               -- scaled marker size
    markerColour          [3] Colour }

DefinedMarkerType ::= INTEGER {
        -- note 0 not allowed
        dot(1),
        plus(2),
        asterisk(3),
        circle(4),
        cross(5)
        }

FillAreaAttribute ::= CHOICE {
        fillBundleIndex       [0] INTEGER (1..MAX),
        interiorStyle         [1] ENUMERATED {
                                  hollow(0),
                                  solid (1),
                                  pattern(2),
                                  hatch(3),
                                  empty(4) },
        fillColour            [2] Colour,
        hatchIndex            [3] INTEGER,
            -- note 0 not allowed
        patternIndex          [4] INTEGER (1..MAX),
        edgeBundleIndex       [5] INTEGER (1..MAX),
        edgeType              [6] DefinedLineType,
```

```
     edgeWidth               [7] CHOICE {
                                 absValue [0] CHOICE {
          -- absolute edge width
                                   [0] INTEGER,
                                -- for integer VDCtype
                                   [1] REAL },
                                -- for real VDCtype
                                 scaled [1] REAL },
         -- scaled edgeWidth
    edgeColour                [8] Colour,
    edgeVisibility            [9] ENUMERATED {
                                   off(0),
                                   on(1) },
    fillReferencePoint        [10] CHOICE {
                                     integerPoint
                                       [0] IntegerPoint,
                                     realPoint
                                       [1] RealPoint },
    patternTable              [11] SEQUENCE {
                                     patternTableIndex
                                       [0] INTEGER (1..MAX),
                                     arrayDimensions
                                       [1] SEQUENCE SIZE (2) OF
                                           INTEGER,
                              note localColourPrecision omitted
                                     patternColourSpecifier
                                       [3] ColourArray },
 patternSize                  [12] CHOICE {
                                     patternVectorsInt
                                       [0] SEQUENCE SIZE (4) OF
                                           INTEGER,
                                     -- integer VDCtype
                                     patternVectorsReal
                                       [1] SEQUENCE SIZE (4) OF
                                           REAL
                                     -- real VDCtype
                                          }
                              }

 ColourTable ::=  SEQUENCE {
    startingIndex             [0] INTEGER,
    colourList                [1] SEQUENCE OF RGB }

 AspectSourceFlags ::= SEQUENCE OF SEQUENCE {
    aspect                    [0] ENUMERATED {
                                  lineTypeASF(0),
                                  lineWidthASF(1),
                                  lineColourASF(2),
                                  markerTypeASF(3),
```

```
                                          markerSizeASF(4),
                                          markerColourASF(5),
                                          interiorStyleASF(6),
                                          fillColourASF(7),
                                          hatchIndexASF(8),
                                          patternIndexASF(9),
                                          edgeTypeASF(10),
                                          edgeWidthASF(11),
                                          edgeColourASF(12) },
        asfvalue                      [1] ENUMERATED {
                                          individual(0),
                                          bundled(1) }
                                          }

    -- Utility types, used in a number of other CGM types

    Colour ::= CHOICE {
        indexed    [0] INTEGER,   -- indexed colour
        direct     [1] RGB }      -- direct colour

    RGB ::= SEQUENCE {
        red        [0] REAL (0..1),
        green      [1] REAL (0..1),
        blue       [2] REAL (0..1) }

    VDCRectangle ::= CHOICE {
                   [0] SEQUENCE {  -- for integer VDCtype
         firstCorner     [0] IntegerPoint,
         secondCorner    [1] IntegerPoint },
                   [1] SEQUENCE {  -- for real VDCtype
         firstCorner     [0] RealPoint,
         secondCorner    [1] RealPoint }
                         }

    PointList ::= CHOICE {
        integerPointList [0] SEQUENCE SIZE (1..MAX)
                              OF IntegerPoint,
        realPointList    [1] SEQUENCE SIZE (1..MAX)
                              OF RealPoint }

    IntegerPoint ::= SEQUENCE {
        x-coordinate [0] INTEGER,
        y-coordinate [1] INTEGER }

    RealPoint ::= SEQUENCE {
        x-coordinate [0] REAL,
        y-coordinate [1] REAL }
```

```
PointEdgePairList ::= CHOICE {
    integerPointEdgePairList [0] SEQUENCE SIZE (1..MAX)
                                 OF IntegerPointEdgePair,
    realPointEdgePairList    [1] SEQUENCE SIZE (1..MAX)
                                 OF RealPointEdgePair
    }

IntegerPointEdgePair ::= SEQUENCE {
    integerPoint [0] IntegerPoint,
    edgeOutFlag  [1] EdgeOutFlag }

RealPointEdgePair ::= SEQUENCE {
    realPoint    [0] RealPoint,
    edgeOutFlag  [1] EdgeOutFlag }

EdgeOutFlag ::= ENUMERATED {
     invisible (0),
     visible (1),
     closeInvisible (2),
     closeVisible (3) }

END
```

Appendix 4 – Contributors to the Project Work

The table below lists the individuals in each organization who contributed to the project work.

Prime Contractor	Thomson-CSF	J.-J. Bardyn
		J. Bisser
		C. Boutillier
		L. Chevalier
		R. Garcia
		L. Mistral
		M. Ramart
		P. Tabastot
		M. Vernay
Partners	COSI	A. Caccia
		E. Gottardi
		E. Paoletti
		E. Paolillo
		E. Pelucchi
		P. Volpato
	GMD-FOKUS	P. Egloff
		C. Fuhrhop
		E. Moeller
		G. Schürmann
		J. Steffens
		St. Wasserroth
	Hitec	P. Kokkinidis
		M. Loupis
	INRIA	A. Ducrot
		C. Hieaux
		M. Planes

	RAL	J.J.S. Cullen
		R.A. Day
		D.A. Duce
		J.R. Gallop
		K. Goswell
		R. Maybury
		D.C. Sutcliffe
	Tecsiel	P. Artico
		F. Dilonardo
		M. Re
Associated Partners	Laser-Scan	R. Fairbairns
		P. Hardy
	FhG-IGD	S. Noll
		J. Rix
	GESI	D. Bovet
		L. Moltedo (Consultant)
	University of East Anglia	D.B. Arnold
		H. Wang
		G.J. Reynolds

Appendix 5 – Publications and Contributions

Publications arising from the project are listed below.

1. D.B. Arnold, D.A. Duce, and D.C. Sutcliffe (1990), "Report on the EUROGRAPHICS/ARGOSI workshop on Graphics and Networking", *Computer Graphics Forum* **9**(4), pp.385-387.
2. D.B. Arnold and D.A. Duce (1990), *ISO Standards for Computer Graphics: The First Generation,* Vol. 1 in Computer Graphics Standards Reference Series, Butterworth's Scientific.
3. D.B. Arnold, R.A. Day, D.A. Duce, C. Fuhrhop, J.R. Gallop, R. Maybury, and D.C. Sutcliffe (1991), *Graphics and Communications,* EurographicSeminars, Springer-Verlag.
4. D.B. Arnold, S.Th. Liapakis, G.J. Reynolds, and N.P. Vezirgiannis (1991), "Practical Considerations in Transporting CGMs", *Computer Aided Design* **23**(4), Butterworth-Heinemann.
5. D.B. Arnold, S.Th. Liapakis, G.J. Reynolds, and N.P. Vezirgiannis (1991), "Transporting CGMs between Implementations – Some Practical Considerations", in *Graphics and Communications*, ed. D.B. Arnold et al., EurographicSeminars, Springer-Verlag. Presented at the First ARGOSI Workshop, 13-15 October 1990
6. J.-J. Bardyn et al. (November 1991), "The ARGOSI Project for ISO/IEC Graphics and Networking Standards", *ESPRIT '91 Conference Proceedings.*
7. J.-J. Bardyn (February 1992), "ARGOSI – Reseaux de Communications et Integrations de Normes", *Thomson HEBDO, nr.379.*
8. R.A. Day, D.A. Duce, A. Ducrot, J.R. Gallop, E. Paollilo, G.J. Reynolds, and D.C. Sutcliffe (1990), "ARGOSI – The Integration of Graphics and Networking", *Proceedings of the Graphics and Interaction in Esprit Sessions, Eurographics '90 Conference, Montreux*, Eurographics Association.
9. D.A. Duce and G.J. Reynolds (May 1990), "Contribution to the UK comments on the Computer Graphics Reference Model", in CGRM – UK Position to Ottawa, BSI doc., no, IST/31: 240.
10. D.A. Duce, J.R. Gallop, G.J. Reynolds, and D.C. Sutcliffe (eds) (1991), "Third Deliverable: Report on Classification", Esprit II Project 2463, ARGOSI. Distributed to ISO/IEC JTC1 SC24 and SC21.

11. P. Egloff (November 1991), "ARGOSI – Applications Related Graphics and OSI Standards Integration", *Meeting of the Graphics Coordination Committee of German Research Institutions*, KFA, Jülich.
12. J.R. Gallop (1991), "The ARGOSI Classification Scheme for Graphics and Networking Applications", in *Graphics and Communications*, ed. D.B. Arnold et al., EurographicSeminars, Springer-Verlag.
13. P. Kokkinidis, M. Loupis, and B. Dimitriadis (May 1991), "Use of standards in the transfer of graphics through computer networks,", *proceedings of 3rd National Informatics Conference*, pp.342-257, Athens, in Greek.
14. M. Loupis and P. Kokkinidis (April-May 1990), "Graphics Applications and Computer Networks", *News Bulletin of the Greek Computer Society* (34), pp.38-43, in Greek.
15. G.J. Reynolds and D.B. Arnold "Mappings between CGI and X", Eurographics '89, State of the Art technical report series. Also available as an AGOCG (Advisory Group on Computer Graphics) Technical Report no. 1.
16. G.J. Reynolds and D.B. Arnold (1991), "CGI profiles for use with X,", in *Graphics and Communications*, ed. D.B. Arnold et al., EurographicSeminars, Springer-Verlag. Presented at the First ARGOSI Workshop, 13-15 October 1990
17. D.C. Sutcliffe, J.R. Gallop, R. Maybury, D.A. Duce, and G.J. Reynolds (1991), "The ARGOSI Classification Scheme for Graphics and Networking Applications", in *Graphics Research & Development in European Community Programmes*, ed. J. Encarnacao, Eurographics Technical Report EG91 G R&D (ISSN 1017-4656).
18. – (December 1991), "Computer Graphics Interfacing techniques for dialogues with graphical devices (CGI) parts 1-6", ISO/IEC 9636.

Printing: Weihert-Druck GmbH, Darmstadt
Binding: Buchbinderei Schäffer, Grünstadt